# MODEL DETECTIVE

## A TRUE STORY OF HEELS, HANDCUFFS AND HOMICIDES

## MICHELE WOOD

**WILD**BLUE
PRESS

**WildBluePress.com**

*MODEL DETECTIVE published by:*
*WILDBLUE PRESS*
*P.O. Box 102440*
*Denver, Colorado 80250*

*Publisher Disclaimer: Any opinions, statements of fact or fiction, descriptions, dialogue, and citations found in this book were provided by the author, and are solely those of the author. The publisher makes no claim as to their veracity or accuracy, and assumes no liability for the content.*



*WILDBLUE PRESS is registered at the U.S. Patent and Trademark Offices.*

*ISBN 978-1-970361-11-7 Hardcover*
*ISBN 978-1-970361-12-4 Trade Paperback*
*ISBN 978-1-970361-10-0 eBook*

*Cover photo courtesy of Officer Frank Alatorre.*
*Cover design © 2026 WildBlue Press. All rights reserved.*

*Interior Formatting and Book Cover Design by Elijah Toten*
*www.totencreative.com*

# MODEL
## DETECTIVE

*For my daughter, who changed everything.*

# ACKNOWLEDGMENTS

Some people change the trajectory of your life simply by opening a door and stepping aside.

Lieutenant D.P.W. was one of those people. One of the finest detectives I have ever known—he gave me a chance when it mattered most, placing me on a homicide team and trusting me to do the work. That decision altered the course of my career, and I have never forgotten it.

Antonia Felix believed in this story before anyone else even knew there was a story. When the idea was still unformed, she recognized its weight and its potential. She helped me understand not just how to write a book, but how to tell the truth on the page—clearly, deliberately, and without apology.

Commander Gary Yamashiroya changed my life in an unscripted moment. During a press conference announcing a murder arrest, with cameras rolling, he paused and said, "Michele can explain it better than anyone."

He called me forward and gave me the floor. That brief moment of trust, offered without rehearsal or expectation, quietly opened the door to a television career I never set out to pursue.

To Area 4—Team Wood—some of the best detectives in this city. Your grit, loyalty, humor, and quiet excellence inspire me every day. You remind me why this work matters—and why I have faith the city will be in good hands long after I'm gone.

And finally, to my mother, Wanda Pena. Our relationship was complicated and challenging, but she remains unforgettable. In time, I came to understand that she loved in the only way she knew how. What I carry forward—strength, resilience, and the resolve to become something more—was shaped as much by what was missing as by what was given.

*Some names and details have been changed or withheld to protect the privacy of those involved.*

# CHAPTER 1

## SUMMERS IN A SQUAD CAR

The first police siren I ever knew wasn't in Chicago—it was my grandfather slapping one of those old-school magnetic gumball lights onto the roof of his blue Chevy Suburban in small-town Terry, Montana back in the '80s. In seconds, his clunky SUV was transformed into a patrol vehicle, and I got my first lesson in what it meant to be the law.

Every summer, my mother packed my sisters Natalie and Melissa and me into a yellow taxi cab and headed to Union Station to board the Amtrak train called the Empire Builder for the long ride west. The farther the train carried us, the more Chicago and everything that came with it drifted away. By the time we reached Wolf Point, Montana, Chicago felt like another planet. My grandfather Eugene Diego Pena was the chief of police in Terry, the kind of chief who knew everyone's name and could settle most problems with a stern look.

My grandfather was married to a woman named Diane, whom I guess I could refer to as my step-grandmother even though she seemed way too young for that title. Their history was quite complex, but I had no idea about that when I was a kid. All I knew was this was my happy place. I waited all year for summertime, when I could escape Chicago and head to Big Sky Country.

My grandfather was a tall, stoic individual who wore a big cowboy hat and had very little emotion unless he was talking to his daughter Gina, who was, coincidentally, one year older than me. My grandfather was much older than his wife, so it was no surprise when they ended up having two children together, my aunt Gina and uncle David. David was one year younger than me, so I referred to him as my cousin to make things easier. I was what they called a "tomboy" back then. I ran around wearing dresses while I climbed trees and rode dirt bikes. My mother made sure I always had shorts underneath in case I decided to climb a fence or chase a suspect… a pretend one. It wasn't really about modesty; it was all about freedom to do whatever I wanted while still being a "lady."

My grandfather and his young family lived in a charming, small-town type of neighborhood in a big, yellow house one house from the corner. It was the same type of house you would see scattered across Montana. This meant vinyl siding, a big, screened in-porch that kept out the mosquitos or "skeeters," as my grandfather referred to them. It did allow a nice breeze in while we played with the boxes of toys that were stored there. Terry, Montana was known for its big sky and the horrific mosquitos that fed on me all summer.

The house sat quietly under an endless sky, weathered and sun-faded, but solid. It was strong enough to last through the wind and dust that came with the brutal summers and equally through the snow in the brutal winters. It was equipped with a screen door that slammed when it closed. Terry was a small town akin to the towns you see in Hallmark movies, the ones that you wonder if they really exist. One bank, one hardware store, and one gas station. Life was simple, and I loved it.

Most of my days were spent going to the local swimming pool down the street, the one my sister and "cousins" walked barefoot to. Other days were spent bike riding into the prairie, the rugged terrain that made me feel free. I didn't have this freedom in Chicago. I wasn't even allowed to play outside most of the time. I remember one time when my mom did allow me to play outside with my neighbors who lived upstairs. We decided to head to the church parking lot, which was right across the street, with the rest of the kids in the neighborhood. We would play kick the can and skateboard while other kids rode their bikes. It was literally the typical 1980s childhood fun that people my age love to reminisce about. Well, I wasn't outside for more than thirty minutes when I literally got run over by an overgrown, manic twelve-year-old boy on a bike. I was so scared my mom would kill him that I hid it from her. I got up and said I was okay. The problem was that I was actually not okay. The kid had plowed me down with a Huffy dirt bike. He'd stopped for a second to tell me he was sorry, although he didn't seem too concerned because he jumped back on the bike and rode away. I tried to brush it off, but I was in some serious pain. This type of "pretending" seemed to continue throughout my youth and into adulthood.

Not long after this, a few days later, I was taking a bath and my mom walked in without knocking. She was shocked to see the enormous bruise that covered the left side of my leg and body, which included tire marks embedded in my skin. She looked concerned for a minute, but the look of shock quickly left her face when she saw me trying to grab a towel to cover myself. Then she was just pissed at me for not telling her. She drilled me for what seemed like hours until I told her what had happened. So, you can imagine why escaping to Montana was so exciting to me.

My grandfather always drove us around town in his Chevy Suburban, the smell of dust and pine and what I can only call the scent of "summer" floating through the windows. When he slipped into "cop mode," I watched him closely—his posture changed, and the car itself seemed to take on authority once those flashing red and blue lights were perched on top. To a little girl, it felt like magic. I also felt a deep sense of pride.

One day, Grandpa brought my older sister Natalie and me to the town jail, and I'll never forget it. It didn't look like the concrete lockups I would later come to know in Chicago. This one belonged in a western movie, with thick bars, heavy keys, and a drain on the floor but no toilet in sight. I remember peering inside the cells, half-expecting an outlaw in a cowboy hat to show his face. Natalie was obviously not as impressed as I was, but her name is Natalie Wood, after all. My mom swore that she got the inspiration for Natalie's name from an old '70s television show called *Romper Room*, and I always believed her until I got older and realized who Natalie Wood was. There's no way she didn't jump on the chance of having a daughter named Natalie Wood. That's, like, one step away from Marilyn Monroe. As I write this, I'm secretly jealous I didn't get the name Natalie Wood. Detective Natalie Wood has such a cooler ring to it than Michele Wood.

Those summers in Montana were the first time I saw police work up close and personal, albeit a different type of policing that is done in Chicago... It wasn't the chaos of sirens screaming through Chicago streets; it was quieter, almost old-fashioned. But it planted something in me which I can only consider a calling.

What I didn't know then was that the world I would return to, the one waiting for me in Chicago, would make my grandfather's little jail look like something out of a storybook. The lessons I learned from him set the foundation for me. My education in what police work really meant was still ahead of me, and it wouldn't be anything like Montana. Not even close.

My childhood shaped me in many ways. My interviewing skills trace back to when I was about eleven years old, though I might have been ten. I have this innate ability to block out things I choose not to think about. As a child, I lived and breathed gymnastics. I went to gymnastics almost every day after school at the local park, Kosciuszko Park, with my best friend Edith. I walked home from gymnastics by myself every night. One evening after returning home from gymnastics practice, my mom asked my sister Natalie and me to run to the GroceryLand store down the street for a case of soda. Back then, Coca-Cola came in twelve-ounce glass bottles. When you finished them, you had to bring the empties back to the store to get your deposit refunded—or else pay an extra sixty or eighty cents.

My sister didn't feel like going. She moaned some version of "no" even after my mom insisted she go with me, so I offered to go alone. I remember exactly what I was wearing that night: a gray jacket, turquoise stretch pants, and my white Pro-Wing brand gym shoes from Payless Shoe Source. We lived on the third floor of a three-story apartment building in the West Logan Square neighborhood in Chicago. It was just my mom, my two sisters Natalie and Melissa, and me at the time. My youngest sister Samantha was years away from existence at this point. Back then, the Logan Square neighborhood wasn't the mecca of shopping and restaurants that it's known for now. Logan Square was more known for poverty and an excessive number of gangs and subsequent wars over gang and narcotics territories.

As soon as I made it down to the ground level and pushed the hallway door open, a middle-aged Hispanic man approached me out of nowhere and asked if I knew where "Jose" lived. I didn't pay him much attention as I walked past him and replied "no" in the sweetest voice I could muster, and I kept walking and headed down the alley toward the grocery store, which was only a block away. I was always very concerned about being polite, so I made sure there was no hint of rudeness to the stranger looking for help. I'm not sure where I got that from, because my mom was a lot of things, but polite wasn't one of them. It was fall—maybe November—and the air had that kind of crisp bite that wakes you up the second you walk outside. The kind that smells faintly of dampness and cold pavement. I was comfortable walking through my neighborhood. I knew its sounds, its shortcuts, its moods. I knew what parts were generally safe. But more importantly, I knew where not to go. I had street smarts even at that young age. That was something I'd always prided myself on. When I got back home about fifteen or twenty minutes later, darkness had already settled in. The streetlights were on, but they didn't do much to illuminate the alley. Their glow barely reached the cracked sidewalks or the narrow side streets. The air was still, and I remember the faint hum of the lamps above the church which was right across the street, and the way my own footsteps echoed off the old brick walls.

I opened the front door to my building—the one with dents and black shoe scuff marks at the bottom from years of being kicked in by quarreling lovers and frustrated tenants who'd forgotten their keys. It was the kind of building that had history in its walls, the kind you could feel if you listened close enough.

The hallway light flickered, and I started up the stairs, taking them two at a time like I always did, my arm wrapped around a heavy case of Coca-Cola Classic. I can still remember the cold metal from the door handle biting into my palms, my breath quick and even. I wasn't thinking about much—probably what I was going to eat for dinner. It was an ordinary moment.

And then, in an instant, it wasn't.

A hand grabbed me from behind, right between my legs—rough, sudden, shocking. My mind couldn't make sense of it fast enough. Before I could even react, I was yanked backward and dragged down the stairs. The Coke case slammed into my leg, but somehow I didn't let go. I was too stunned to scream. I tried to get out the words— "Let me go!"—but what came out was barely a whisper, strangled by fear.

Even now, all these years later, I can still feel the confusion more than the pain, the disbelief that this was actually happening. That someone had taken my sense of safety and shattered it in a single motion.

Somewhere in the middle of that chaos, instinct kicked in. I twisted and fought with everything I had. My turquoise pants ripped at the seam. Somehow, I broke free. I stumbled back into the dim hallway light, shaking, breathless, still clutching that heavy case of soda like it was the only thing tethering me to reality.

I ran up all forty stairs to our apartment, counting each step as I ran up, and began pounding on the door with everything I had. I could hear my sister's television program blaring inside, but it felt like forever before someone opened the door. When my mom finally answered, she took one look at my tears and didn't need to hear much more. All I could choke out was, "Some guy tried to grab me."

Without hesitation, she grabbed the first thing she could find—a bat, a stick, maybe even a shovel—and charged down the stairs, ready to face whoever had touched her child. Moments later, the police arrived and soon, detectives from Chicago Police Area Five were there too. They questioned me for hours and promised that they would find this predator.

The truth was, I couldn't describe him. I didn't have answers to most of their questions. There were details I did know, but they never asked me about those things. I never got a chance to tell them. I knew the stranger's flannel shirt was damp, like he'd just risen from underneath a car, lying on damp, recently rained on pavement. I knew he smelled like oil and engines. I knew he was dirty and needed a bath. It wasn't the smell of a homeless person; it was the smell of someone who had been working all day. I knew he seemed comfortable, like he belonged in the neighborhood. I even believed his car was parked across the street, though I couldn't explain how I knew that—maybe I'd seen him near it before he spoke to me. Maybe I'd seen him there before.

I'm not sure. The detectives asked me to show them how he pulled me down the stairs.

I said, "He grabbed my arm," and I proceeded to try to show them how that could have happened. I was embarrassed to tell them the truth. The odd thing was I didn't know why I was embarrassed. It wasn't like I'd done something that caused this to happen, right? I wanted them to catch the fact that I was holding back, but they never did. I would have countless meetings with them for what seemed like every day after school, to look at big books of mug shots to try to figure out who had done this. I wonder if they ever knew his motive. I didn't then, but I do now.

At that age, I didn't understand what he was trying to do. When he pulled at my pants, I didn't even know what a sexual assault was. I only knew I was terrified. In my mind, I saw my face on the back of a milk carton, like the missing kids I stared at every morning at breakfast. I assumed he was trying to kidnap me.

That night, after the man attacked me, I went into my room and sewed my ripped pants back together. I remember staring at the white, milky stain on the fabric—unsure what it was, but knowing it was bad. I felt ashamed, disgusted, and far too young to even put words to it.

After the incident, I tried to act like that attack didn't bother me, though inside it haunted me. I never told my mom the full truth of what had happened. I knew she couldn't take it, and part of me believed it would break her heart beyond repair. Plus, I didn't want to relive it and if my mom knew, she would never let it go.

From that day forward, I made a plan: if I ran everywhere I went, no one could ever grab me again. A moving target would be harder to catch. So that's what I did. I ran. I ran to school, I ran to the store, I ran up and down our stairwell. I ran as if my life depended on it.

I'm only able to share this complete story now, years later, because my mother has passed away. Even as an adult, I truly believe that telling her what really happened would have broken her in a slow, irreversible way. After the detectives stopped showing up at our house and moved on to the next case, we never spoke about it again.

Instead, my mother did what she could in silence. She bought me a small can of mace, though it wasn't even called that. The label read "Protect You Aid," a name that gave me some reassurance. I carried it everywhere, clenched in my hand, my fingers wrapped tightly around the red plastic cap like it was a lifeline. It became my constant companion, held at the ready, a quiet reminder that I was no longer carefree.

This incident took away some of my innocence. It changed me. From then on, I started learning how to read people, how to stay alert, and how to walk with confidence, so no one mistook me for easy prey again.

Later, as a detective, I tried numerous times to get ahold of the original case file to see if the detectives ever had any leads. The guy was never caught. A few months after the attack, I learned that my classmate Maryann, the girl who lived on the second floor and who was the same age as me, was attacked and sexually assaulted in the alley behind our house. I'm pretty sure it was the same guy. Police have a saying: "No face, no case." And I didn't have a face. But I never forgot the man I couldn't describe.

# CHAPTER 2

# THE TRUTH SHALL SET YOU FREE

I ended up going to Lane Tech High School, which carried a certain reputation back then. It was known as a really good school, the kind of school that people were proud to get in to. Smart kids. High expectations. They used to joke and call us "Lane Brains."

For me, it felt like going from being a big fish in a small pond to completely unnoticeable overnight.

At Lane, I disappeared. Not because I wasn't capable, but because I wasn't focused, and honestly, I didn't care. My life outside school was loud and unstable, and none of that fit neatly into a classroom. Home wasn't a place where homework got done. There were too many of us crammed into a small Chicago apartment, and I didn't even have a bedroom. I slept on the couch when I was there at all.

Most Fridays, my mom kicked me out for the weekend. This constant chaos was enough to keep me unsteady. I bounced between two friends' houses, basically living there. A spare bed was better than the couch waiting for me, and at least I didn't feel like I was in the way.

So, school became something I got through, not something I invested in. I cut class. I learned how to blend into hallways and do just enough to stay under the radar. Lane Tech was a great school but just not for me.

I graduated by doing the bare minimum.

My survival took precedence over success. While other kids were thinking about college, I was thinking about where I was sleeping and how to stay invisible.

By the time graduation came, college never felt like an option. because no one had ever shown me that it was an option. No one in my family had gone. There were no campus tours, no guidance counselors walking us through applications, no conversations about majors or futures that came with syllabi. My mom would have supported anything I chose—she always did—but encouragement toward college wasn't part of our world. You did what you could with what you had, and you figured the rest out as you went. What I needed wasn't a campus. It was structure. Direction. A way out.

So, when I graduated high school, I did what made sense at the time. I joined the United States Army.

I joined because I needed direction, structure, and a way forward. The army gave me all three. It gave me discipline before I even knew I needed it. It taught me how to show up on time, how to follow orders, how to lead when it was my turn, and how to keep going when quitting would have been easier.

When my stint on active duty ended, I stayed in the reserves for six years. One weekend a month, every month, no excuses. I learned early how to balance two worlds: the one where people saw me, and the one where I quietly carried obligations no one else had to understand.

That duality would follow me for the rest of my life.

I also had some savings for the first time in my life, and it felt good. I was always afraid of being broke, so having that small sense of security mattered to me. This is where the hustle started. I became an aerobics instructor, standing on a platform under fluorescent lights, counting reps and shouting encouragement over loud music. I bartended. I waitressed. I worked at a lamp manufacturer as an office manager, all while I went to school full-time and drilled with the Army Reserves once a month. And I did all of these jobs at the same time. My job depended on what day it was.

Those years were a blur of early mornings and late nights, uniforms traded for leggings, aprons, or name tags, depending on the shift. I learned how to read people fast. I knew who was going to tip well, who wanted to be left alone, who needed conversation more than a drink. I learned how to manage chaos, multitask under pressure, and stay calm when things went awry.

I didn't know it then, but I was training for police work long before I ever took the police entry exam.

There's something humbling about working that many jobs while trying to build something bigger. You constantly feel tired, but you also feel capable. You learn that you can survive on very little sleep, that you can adapt, that you can handle more than you thought. I wasn't wandering aimlessly; I was collecting tools.

I just didn't know yet how important these tools would be to me later in life.

Then came what I thought was the dream job.

I was hired as a flight attendant with Southwest Airlines, and I was thrilled. The uniform, the travel, the energy… it felt exciting and different and full of possibility. I'd made it into something people admired. Something that sounded impressive when you said it out loud.

For a while, I loved it.

But somewhere between the flights and the routines, I felt that familiar feeling again. I call it quiet restlessness I'd learned not to ignore. I liked the job, but I didn't love the life. I knew, deep down, that I was still searching for something better. Something more "me." Something harder. Something that mattered in a way I couldn't fully explain yet.

So, in August of 2000, I took the Chicago Police Department exam.

I didn't overthink it. I didn't romanticize it. I just knew. The process moved quickly. I was fast-tracked, and on February 5, 2001, I officially joined the Chicago Police Department Academy.

Looking back, it all makes sense. The army. The discipline. The hustle jobs. The customer service. The travel. Every step sharpened me for what came next. I didn't arrive at policing by accident. I arrived prepared.

I just didn't yet know how deeply it would change me.

***

I was promoted to detective very early, after just five years on the job. At the time, the average number of years it took to make detective was at least ten, and many had over thirty years on the job when they moved up. Imagine getting promoted after thirty years? No thanks. I would be planning my escape.

My first assignment as a detective was working in the Special Victims Unit in Area One, where I handled domestic-related crimes on the South Side of Chicago. I worked with a crew of hard chargers: Tony, Jarred, and Pam. Pam reminded me of a modern day Foxy Brown. My tenure on the South Side lasted less than a year before I bid out and transferred to Area Three's Bureau of Detectives on the North Side of Chicago, which was closer to home. This is where I started working sex crimes and increasingly more violent crimes until I reached homicide. Area Three is where I teamed up with my partner John Korolis. John and I knew each other from our previous assignment as police officers in the Targeted Response Unit before we were promoted to detective, so it was an easy decision to pair up with him temporarily. He would end up being my partner for over ten years. We handled every type of sex case you can imagine.

Working sex crimes will change you. There's something uniquely haunting about sexual assault cases. They're not only crimes of violence, but they're violations of the soul. The aftermath doesn't end when a report is filed or even when the bad guy is arrested or convicted. The aftermath requires the victim to live with the trauma and somehow try to rebuild from it.

The reality hit me hardest in the case of Tina Gerber, a young woman who was viciously assaulted steps away from her home. It was a regular, rather uneventful day working Violent Crimes. John and I had just finished dinner when we got the call. We were assigned to a sexual assault that had just occurred, and as luck would have it, we were eating close by. All we were told was that a sexual assault of a woman had happened on a cement parking pad behind a million-dollar home near the Wrigleyville neighborhood.

We arrived at the crime scene and were immediately met by a thirty-something-year-old man with light brown hair and a buzz cut. He was obviously a cop, judging by the ballistic vest he wore over his clothing. He was pacing back and forth, clearly upset. We learned that he was the victim's boyfriend. I could tell he wasn't a Chicago Police officer. Maybe it comes from the fact that after a first few months on the job, Chicago officers are exposed to more real-life trauma than most people see in a lifetime. The city has a way of reshaping you quickly. Experience settles into your body before you even realize it's happening. It impacts how you stand, how you scan a room, how you hold yourself without thinking about it. It isn't something you're taught so much as something you absorb just by being there.

This guy didn't have that. His posture was stiff, his movements slightly delayed, like he was concentrating on looking the part instead of simply being it. Chicago cops don't perform authority; it's natural. It's not the exaggerated stance you see on *Chicago P.D.* It's quieter and immediate, though I do get a kick out of the *Chicago P.D.* TV show.

They obviously use a real-life CPD advisor for the scripts. So, from experience alone, I knew he couldn't be CPD. And I was correct. He explained that he was an off-duty police officer from an unincorporated suburb miles from Chicago. He explained that there were only a handful of officers in his department, which meant that on an average day, he could go from being the evidence technician to the traffic officer to the watch commander—depending on the day and how many officers were working.

He was standing outside the back door of his residence, which was a short distance from the actual crime scene. John and I introduced ourselves, and he gave us the basic facts of what had occurred. He was off today and was getting everything ready for Christmas. He'd taken a break on the couch to watch some TV when he got a text on his cell phone from his longtime girlfriend, now fiancée, Tina that read: "I'm being raped in the alley." He went on to say he thought she was "joking."

Now, I'll be honest: I have a pretty dark sense of humor that I consider an occupational hazard from the work I do. It's almost a job requirement. But I could never imagine joking about something like that.

I probably gave him a perplexed look as I asked him if she normally joked about things like this, and he quickly said, "No, never." He explained that when the text came in, he was sitting on the couch watching a movie. He didn't have socks on, so for whatever reason he chose not to go outside to check if there was any truth to the message she'd sent. That decision, I'm sure, will haunt him forever.

After finishing that basic interview with the boyfriend, we headed to the actual crime scene, which was located a few houses down the alley. It was on a parking pad in the back of a neighbor's home. A parking pad is just a cement slab where a garage should have been, located in a fairly well-lit alley. It was late December and snow covered the ground in a crusty, uneven layer. You could smell the metallic bite of blood in the frozen air. Blood droplets were scattered in the snow, and there were voids pressed down where warm bodies had been. Officers had already been there for a while, their heavy boots leaving prints all over, but they'd done their best to preserve what they could. After a careful look, we decided to head to Illinois Masonic Medical Center, located just five minutes away, to interview the victim, Tina. We would come back to the scene after we talked to her.

John parked our unmarked beige Chevy Malibu in the ambulance zone at Illinois Masonic and pushed through the sliding glass doors of the emergency room. The fluorescent lights buzzed overhead, the smell of antiseptic hitting us instantly. We were directed toward Tina, who sat in the back of the ER, speaking softly with a doctor.

I asked the questions. John took the notes.

Tina was a pretty, petite twenty-something woman with dark hair, fair skin, and blue eyes, who had been on her way home on the CTA Red Line from work. She'd decided to stop at Walgreens on her walk home from the train station for wrapping paper. Christmas was just days away.

She explained that she got off the train and started walking down Belmont Ave., the busy street glowing with holiday lights and traffic noise. It was cold, but not bitter, just the kind of chill where snow glistens under the streetlamps instead of melting. After grabbing the wrapping paper and a few other items, she walked a few blocks, turned left onto her usual street, and headed right into the alley that led to the house she shared with her fiancé.

She told us it was already dark, but the streets were well lit. Even the alley had lights, which made her feel safe enough to walk. She'd probably taken this same route a hundred times before. She turned right and immediately realized she'd made a mistake. A man was behind her, close enough to steal her air. His breath brushed her neck, and then a hard object pressed into her head, which left no doubt about what was coming next.

The man spoke closely, his mouth and hot, stale breath inches away from her face, and ordered her to empty her pockets. She thought he would take her things and leave. That's what she was praying for, but he didn't. Instead, he pushed her to an area hidden from passersby, violently yanked down her pants, and forced her onto the frozen cement slab of the parking pad. The cold bit into her skin as tried to force himself inside her. Tina didn't want to die, so she didn't fight back. When the attacker couldn't perform in the freezing air, his frustration turned to rage. He forced her to perform degrading sexual acts. He then beat her savagely. shattering her nose and orbital bone. She said he barked, "Sit on my face," and again, she complied, knowing that her life was hanging by a thread.

She politely asked him if she could pick up some snow to put on her battered face to stop the bleeding, and he obliged. While he was distracted, she managed to slip her phone from her front pocket. Instead of calling 911, she sent a text: "I'm being raped in the alley."

Her boyfriend never came.

Somehow, bloodied and bruised, Tina escaped. She left with her strength intact and her aggressor's DNA. I've never met another victim as calm as Tina. In fact, one officer in the ER even questioned her story because of how steady she was. But I knew she was telling the truth. That kind of calm doesn't come from confusion or shock; it comes from control. It's someone who has decided not to unravel in front of strangers. She wasn't detached from what happened; she was managing it, using composure as a way to take her power back.

I promised Tina that I would get the person who had done this to her. And I kept my promise. That promise also came with a full confession from the predator, a plea of guilty, and zero remorse. His name was Tyrone, and he was a convicted felon who was on house arrest. He was living at a halfway house not far from the crime scene. He'd actually just been recently released by a too accommodating judge who didn't think he was a threat to society. He was out and about, trying to make the most of his day before his mandated 8:00 p.m. curfew. He actually told me that he'd only planned to rob Tina, but when he saw how scared she was, he decided to rape her too. He said he was watching her while he was "looking for a victim."

She caught his attention as he crossed paths with Tina while walking in the opposite direction on Belmont Ave. He stopped to see where she was going to go. When she turned down the alley, he decided that she would be his victim. Tina might have caught a glimpse of him, but she had no idea he was watching her and planning his next move based on hers. It was a sick game of chess for him.

He told me when she decided to proceed down the alley, it was "the wrong turn for her and the right turn for me." This statement hit me like a ton of bricks. How I wished she would have gone another way. But he'd made up his mind. After all, he was looking for a victim… exactly like he said. If it wasn't Tina, it would have been someone else. He said he used a mini Bible that he got from the county jail from one of those prison ministries and put it up to her head so she would think it was a gun. After that interview, I warned every woman I knew about the importance of judging a book by its cover. And I wasn't saying don't do it. Quite the contrary. Women are taught to ignore our instincts, to be polite, to give people the benefit of the doubt. Tina did exactly that. She sensed something was wrong, thought he might have been following her, but convinced herself she was overreacting.

When your safety is on the line, politeness is a liability. You don't owe anyone comfort at the expense of your own instincts. I learned that lesson once… and I repeat, only once. You can always apologize later if you're wrong. But if you're right, hesitation can cost you everything.

The Assistant State's Attorney came out and took a handwritten confession from him. She sat across the table, pen moving steadily across the paper as he described what he'd done in detail—maybe even reliving it, but her face gave her away. Even after years in the State's Attorney's office and after hearing from the worst versions of humanity, she was visibly shocked.

What horrified all of us wasn't just what he admitted to; it was how easily the words came. There was no hesitation, no searching for language, and no visible weight to the things he described. He spoke plainly, almost conversationally, as if he were recounting an errand or a routine day. Each sentence landed heavier than the last, filling the room with a silence that felt thick and suffocating. He only left one detail out. It was an important detail, but this was his version of self-preservation. It didn't matter, though.

We'd all been in enough interview rooms to recognize rehearsed lies, deflection, and fear. This wasn't that. This was someone unburdened by conscience, someone who had crossed a line so completely that he no longer recognized it as a line at all. The confession wasn't pulled from him. It didn't have to be. It freely spilled out, unguarded and disturbingly calm.

When it was over, no one spoke right away. The room held onto what had been said, as if the walls themselves needed time to absorb it. We walked out knowing the case was closed on paper, but also knowing that some things you hear never leave you, no matter how many years pass. The State's Attorney hammered him, charging him with a count for each offense and each time he'd assaulted Tina.

Years later, when I hit the stand to testify in a motion to suppress his confession, the slick defense attorney tried to twist something I'd said to the rapist while interviewing him. I'd told him, "The truth shall set you free." I don't know if the presence of the Bible at the attack made me get all biblical, but when I said "free," I was referring to the freedom from running, hiding, and lying, and the freedom from the weight of what he'd done.

In court while being cross-examined, the defense attorney asked me a question that he didn't really expect an answer for. "You told him to tell you the truth and you'd set him free, didn't you?" That was a reminder that words don't always land the way we intend them to. In a courtroom, words can be taken out of context and even weaponized against you. Sometimes, it's intentional. Other times, it's just the nature of high-stakes interviews where you're later subject to being dissected under a microscope.

There aren't many true monsters in the world. Most of what I've seen on this job are flawed people making bad decisions... sometimes terrible ones, but still recognizably human. Tyrone was different. He was a special breed. I haven't encountered many like him. There was no confusion in him, no remorse waiting to be uncovered, and no explanation that softened the edges. What he did wasn't impulsive; it was deliberate, practiced, and empty of hesitation. Some people can be redirected or even saved. Tyrone wasn't one of them—at least not in my opinion. He was a monster, and the danger with men like him is that they look ordinary enough to walk unnoticed among the rest of us.

This predator got a hefty sentence, but not nearly as long as he deserved. One day, he'll be out, and I fear he'll strike again. When I think of resilience and strength, I think of Tina Gerber. And truthfully, I still think about her to this day.

# CHAPTER 3

## THAT ELUSIVE QUALITY

There's an elusive quality every great homicide detective has. It's something you can't quite define, but you know it when you see it. It's the strange alchemy of making people fear you, respect you, and like you, all at the same time.

In the old days, the Chicago Police homicide detective was a good ole boy. His father was on the job, he lived and breathed police work, and he carried himself with a swagger passed down through generations. But policing changed, and so did the detectives. The new breed wasn't born into the job—they earned their way in by outworking everyone, grinding through twenty-four-hour shifts, and spending entire days at the Criminal Courts Building, a place that felt less like a courthouse and more like a dysfunctional family reunion of criminals, witnesses, defense attorneys, prosecutors, and cops.

My own interrogation style came from the thirty random jobs I'd had before the CPD and twenty-five years of watching human behavior the way other people watch Netflix. The first rule: dress like you mean business. In Chicago, you could tell where a detective worked by their shirt alone. Area Four guys wore white shirts with boring ties. Their dress shirts were so thin you could see their undershirts and, unfortunately, their nipples. Area Three favored trendy colors and patterns.

My lieutenant always knew when I was preparing for an interview because I dressed like I was headed to either a job interview or a first date. They sound different, but they require the exact same thing: confidence, strategy, and the ability to make someone want to talk to you.

For women, detective clothes are a different beast. Men throw on dress pants, tuck in a shirt, and holster a gun. Women? We pray the belt loops won't rip off from the weight of the holster, magazines, and handcuffs. We search for outfits that stay tucked, don't bunch, and still allow us to move like we're not wearing a corset made of ballistic nylon.

People assume female detectives flirt during interviews. It's not flirting exactly, it's reading the room, being warm when you need to be, firm when it matters, and always in control. You never give the offender the upper hand. Yelling rarely works. Humans tend to shut down when you scream at them, and in homicide, you only get one shot. So, I do the opposite: I let them talk. I let them explain. I let them feel heard. And then I wait for them to slip up.

If you do it right, the bad guy starts developing something close to Stockholm syndrome. You took his freedom, put him in that room, and you're the only one who can give him a voice. Then you step out, and suddenly he's knocking on the door asking for you, begging for you to come back so he can "tell his side." And the crazy thing? It works. It works a lot. That dynamic doesn't stay locked inside the interview room. Once you understand how quickly power, access, and attention can distort someone's perception, you start seeing it everywhere, including outside of work. Also, if it isn't obvious: never, under any circumstances, date anyone you met investigating a case. Dating an arrestee or a victim isn't edgy or complicated. It's a line only people with poor boundaries and worse judgment even consider crossing.

Plus, you don't want to be the next subject on an episode of *Dateline*.

Dating, as a female homicide detective, is its own kind of crime scene. Different setting, same red flags. After enough years on the job, patterns emerge. The men I encountered fell neatly into three categories:

Men who fetishize cops.

Men who wouldn't touch a cop with a baton.

And the unicorn: confident men who aren't threatened by a woman in power.

Those men exist but only as often as an open parking spot on a Chicago side street.

I grew up on '80s cop shows like *Hunter* and *MacGruder and Loud*, convinced I would be a superhero catching bad guys. My inspiration was Sergeant Rick Hunter, not his partner Dee Dee, who was cool but undeniably second fiddle. I didn't want to be the sidekick. I wanted to be the one kicking down the door.

No offense to Olivia Benson, but outside of *Law & Order*, homicide detectives who are pretty, well-rested, emotionally balanced, and sipping lattes in cashmere sweaters simply don't exist. They're like UFOs… plenty of people claim they've seen one, but nobody has proof.

The job corrected that thinking soon enough. Not just the TV fantasy I grew up believing in, but the bigger myth too—that this work is about heroes.

It isn't.

It hit me one day standing in a high-rise apartment crime scene with my partner John. I reminded myself of the second most important rule after "figure out lunch." A great partner is everything. Someone you trust with your life. Someone who will have your back without question and, equally important in police work, someone you're not sleeping with.

It's about partners.

We weren't Benson and Stabler sharing bodega coffee on a stakeout. In Chicago, it was Dunkin', extra large, half burnt, and always lukewarm. A partner is someone who shares that elusive detective quality, the mix of grit, heart, and presence that makes the job survivable.

Back in the day, becoming a homicide detective took years. Detective exams used to come around maybe once a decade. I took mine in 2003 with precisely 2.5 years on the job, which was the bare minimum to be eligible. That exam produced every new detective until 2012. Entire classes of officers couldn't even apply for nine years.

No one walked straight into homicide. You earned a spot, if you were lucky. When I arrived in Area Three, the average homicide detective had more than thirty years on the job. They didn't let rookies near murders, so John and I learned by showing up, shadowing them, and waiting until sheer exhaustion forced them to go home. That's when we would swoop in and work the case.

The job changed as the years went on. The old guard aged out. Eventually, the homicide detective wasn't a generational legacy, but the person willing to grind harder than anyone else. Willing to live at the Criminal Courts Building. Willing to give the job everything.

After one last walk through the victim's apartment, I slapped a "coroner's seal" on the door, although the real lock on that scene was the victim's keys in my pocket. I turned the key, heard the deadbolt click, and headed off to lunch with John. Because no matter how brutal the case, how elusive the truth, or how long the shift… every detective knows one rule: you can't solve a murder on an empty stomach.

# CHAPTER 4

# THE A-TEAM

Back in 2012, the big bosses in the Chicago Police Department decided it needed to "fix crime." Chicago had been the punchline on late-night TV: pizza, politics, corruption, and murder, always in that order. Tourism was dipping, politicians were panicking, and someone upstairs decided the best solution was to restructure the entire Detective Division.

So… poof! Our five detective areas were collapsed into three. Detectives were ripped out of their neighborhood offices and shipped to the North and South Sides, where morale was low, and the buildings looked like they'd failed inspection in the '70s. No Wi-Fi. No real desks. No working computers. But hey, crime-fighting optics, right? Nothing says "strong police presence" like dumping a bunch of detectives into a crumbling building with no parking spots. To us, it felt like classic smoke and mirrors. But our opinions didn't matter; this was way above our pay grade.

The new structure was simple in theory: detectives would specialize.

- Homicide detectives only worked homicides.

- Sex Crimes detectives stayed in Sex Crimes.

- Robbery/Burglary had their own squad.

Eventually, we were supposed to become experts in our lanes.

In the old days, homicide detectives worked whatever came in. You had your partner, and you would call whomever you trusted for help. No teams. No formality. Just whoever was willing to roll out to a scene with you, knowing there was no end time in sight. Now? We were getting homicide teams.

Each team would ideally be six detectives—three sets of partners—led by their sergeant. Every new homicide rotated who was "up" for a murder: one pair was lead detective, and the others were helpers.

Being lead detective meant you got to bark orders and stroll the crime scene like Kojak with a lollipop. Being helper detective, though? Totally underrated. You showed up, pointed at things with authority, looked important for the news cameras, and when anyone asked a hard question, you just redirected: "You'll have to ask the lead."

Genius, if you ask me.

The announcement day with assignments was coming. People were sweating. Would they end up in Robbery? Burglary? Sex Crimes, AKA "Sexy Detective," as I'd been lovingly (annoyingly) nicknamed? But everyone knew what the overachievers wanted: a spot on Homicide, the major leagues.

Realistically, I figured I might end up back in Sex Crimes, where I'd started, or on the Shooting Team. That's Attempted Homicide, which is close, but not quite the show. The minor leagues. Not the "you suck" minor leagues; more like, "Yeah, I'm kind of pro, but not really."

And while the Shooting Team was respectable, your business cards didn't hit the same.

Honestly, they should have read: "Almost a Homicide Detective."

Shooting victims in Chicago often give the same line: didn't see anything, didn't hear anything, heard a shot, and then felt pain. There should be a checkbox on the interview sheet for "Heard Shot, Felt Pain." That's code for "I'm handling this myself." Today's victim, tomorrow's offender. The circle of life, Chicago-style.

Still, I'd paid my dues. I was ready. Whether with my partner John or not, I wanted in. The guys I would be working with if I made Homicide were a cast of characters straight out of central casting.

Greg, the seasoned vet with the Jekyll-and-Hyde personality, liked to unwind after a homicide by sitting in his basement in his underwear, sipping the cheapest merlot known to man. It tasted so horrible we refused to give it the proper French pronunciation. It was mer-laht.

His partner Marco Garcia—better known as Mr. 312—was our Chicago version of the rapper Pitbull. Puerto Rican, loud, hilarious, and somehow exactly what every room needed the second he walked into it. He had this rare ability to shift effortlessly, a true linguistic chameleon. One minute, he sounded like an inner city Black guy, the next a Hispanic gang member, then a White suburban kid, all without parody or performance. It wasn't calculated. I don't even think he realized he did it. It was based on who his audience was. I think it's officially called code-switching these days. People trusted him because they heard themselves in him. Marco had grown up on the South Side, in a gang-infested neighborhood. His parents quickly moved them to the North Side when they realized his brother Papo was getting all too comfortable with the local gang members.

Marco's skills and Colgate smile allowed doors to open. Tension dropped. It was a superpower, and he wielded it without ever stopping to admire it. I actually went to high school with him, which made the whole partnership feel inevitable. The universe had been quietly lining us up long before either of us knew we would end up here, doing this work, together.

Then there was Art, partnered with JC. Art was too smart to be a police officer, but too into the job to be anywhere else. Sweater vests Monday through Friday. Suspects somehow adored him and readily opened up to him. How threatening could a guy in a sweater vest really be?

JC and I have known each other since we were teenagers. In high school, he dated a few of my closest girlfriends, so I truly consider him a brother of sorts. I was elated when I heard he and his partner were on my team. He would fit in nicely. JC's favorite phrase was, "Can you believe they give us guns and pay us for this?"

When JC was younger, he was quite the ladies' man. He figured if you played the numbers game with girls, someone would eventually say yes. It turns out he was right. JC was no longer playing the field, since he'd gotten married and God blessed him with not one, but two daughters to keep him up late at night in penance for the girls he'd loved and left.

Mike Hammond was also part of the team. He was working solo for the most part and would jump in whenever we needed a little help. Mike was a tough-looking teddy bear with a heart of gold. He was getting ready to retire and would be going to Cold Case soon to finish up his career. Our sergeant was The Big Toe. He was an old-school Irish cop who only answered to "Sergeant." Nobody remembered his first name. Legend has it even his wife called him Sergeant in bed. He spoke sparingly, just enough to keep us in line. If this ended up being my team, I'd hit the jackpot.

The morning the assignments were supposed to be finalized, I was walking to my squad car, mind running in circles, when a guy in a hard hat who looked like he was working for the gas company stopped me. Older Black guy, piercing green eyes. "Hey, baby, where are you going with those curves?"

Sir… absolutely not. Wrong day, wrong audience. I gave him a death stare and kept walking. I checked the back seat as I always do, then got inside. Before you enter a squad car, you're supposed to check the back seat to make sure no one left a concealed bag of dope—or worse, a gun. There have been rumors of Internal Affairs doing random integrity checks for as long as I've been on the job. So, if you find something that doesn't belong to you, you'd better report it. This includes a crisp one-hundred-dollar bill. The consequences could cost you your livelihood and, worst case scenario, your freedom.

The squad car reeked of stale fast food. Some genius had eaten lunch there and smashed the greasy bag under the seat. An extra large 7-Eleven fountain beverage—sweating and disintegrating—overflowed sticky syrup into a makeshift cup holder made from a broken crate stuffed with rolls of crime scene tape. Typical. Probably a guy. And probably proud of himself.

A few nights earlier, sitting at home, I'd thought about how badly I wanted this. I'd wanted to be a homicide detective my whole life. Ever since childhood. Ever since I learned what the job really was. And here's the truth: real homicide work isn't sexy.

You work twenty to thirty hours straight.

You look like hell.

Your marriage disintegrates.

You gain weight because at 3:00 a.m., your only food options are tacos or pancakes.

You start drinking to forget what you can't unsee.

It chips away at you.

The one thing that saves you is a great partner. Someone you trust with your life. Someone who doesn't complicate it. Someone whose spouse doesn't hate you—which in my world is the highest compliment. John's wife actually liked me. That says everything.

So, as messy as the reorganization was, as ridiculous as the politics were, I still wanted that spot.

I'd earned it. I was ready for the A-Team.

# CHAPTER 5

# ALWAYS MATCH YOUR UNDERWEAR

Joining the Homicide Team was a milestone I'd been chasing for years, and when I finally made it, I was equal parts proud and terrified. It's one thing to want something, and another thing entirely when they hand you the badge, the caseload, and the responsibility. When you first land on a homicide team, nobody hands you a manual. As the months went on, I had enough experience to know where the copy paper was, but not enough to not have to consult with my sergeant for advice on which way to go.

I was still figuring out who actually did their job, who needed hand-holding, and who would throw you under a bus without blinking. Homicide is a team sport, sure, but only if you know how the players move. You learn by walking into chaos and pretending you belong there until you actually do. Those first weeks were all about working out the kinks, figuring out who was solid, who talked too much, and who you needed next to you at three in the morning with a body on the floor and a mother screaming in the hallway. I was getting to know the other detectives on my team, the routines, the personalities, and the unwritten rules that mattered more than anything written in a manual. Every case, even the simple ones, felt like a test.

And every so often, a homicide would come through that reminded me I was no longer the new girl. I was starting to hold my own, walking scenes with confidence, trusting my instincts, and learning when to shut up and when to speak up. Little did I know that all of that adjusting, all of that quiet observing, was leading me straight into one of the cases that would stay with me forever: the murder of Yolanda Holmes.

It was an unseasonably warm September day in Chicago, and I was dressed in my typical detective attire. My thin, black cotton dress pants were perfect for the warm weather. In the winter, these same pants don't do a thing to protect me from the freezing wind that literally cuts through them. My tiny black leather jacket made me look tough as hell, or so I was told. But I was literally sweating before I even got in the car. I was wearing black leather comfort pumps and no socks, so my feet were both sweating and freezing from the air conditioning that I had on full blast. Not a fun combination.

I'd just received the call. It's never a good sign when a homicide detective's phone rings during work, or even after work, for that matter. Some detectives would say don't pick up if you see a 744 prefix before your shift. Anytime my phone rings, I get that sinking feeling. It's usually a sign that someone is dead. That would "ring" correct on this day, and I wasn't even on the clock yet.

I learned that a murder had occurred earlier in the day. One of my sergeants, Sergeant Guzman, told me he needed "my expertise." I knew from experience that "my expertise" meant it was some kind of clusterfuck of a case. Sergeant Guzman was a legendary police officer who worked in the 14th District before I got there. He was well liked and used to wear a Superman Under Armour brand shirt underneath his uniform. I'm not sure if this was fact or fiction, but something tells me it was true. Sarge told me that Detective Dan Ortman would be calling me with the details ASAP.

Dan was one of the oldie detectives who worked the phones for his last few years as he got ready for retirement. The usual guy who dispatched the jobs to the detectives, Dan was short on information, as usual. Dan was well known by all of the police officers who called the area with notifications about new reports. He usually gave the police officers who called in about thirty seconds to get their story out before he responded with a barrage of questions. If you didn't have every bit of information handy, you were better off hanging up and calling back before he hung up on you. "Call me back when you figure out what you're doing, Officer!" Dan's time wouldn't be wasted by an unprepared officer. Oh, and all of your preliminary case reports had better be done or you weren't getting a detective sent to you. A self-proclaimed gun aficionado, Dan had lots of guns to clean in between phone calls, and he had no patience for laziness or sloppiness.

Dan said all he could tell me was that a female had been found DOA—dead on arrival—in her bed in her apartment located in the Uptown area in Chicago. The Uptown area is located on the far North Side, close to the Lakefront and the infamous Lake Shore Drive, the fifteen-plus-mile expressway that runs along the shoreline of Lake Michigan, which tourists often call the "Ocean of Chicago" due to its size. Uptown is known as a culturally diverse neighborhood that encompasses the West Argyle Street Historic District, which is also known by the name "Little Saigon" or "Little Vietnam." Uptown is considered a relatively safe area, but it does experience its fair share of crime, including robberies and gang shootings in certain pockets of the area. The Wilson Street CTA Red Line train also runs alongside the neighborhood, which brings its own share of problems.

Many Chicagoans would rather take a longer route to work than risk being a victim of crime on the Red Line, often referred to by commenters on social media as the "Blood Line." But statistically, there aren't a lot of homicides in the Uptown area, so the murders that do occur are usually newsworthy. We could expect this case to be a "heater."

Dan told me he wasn't sure if the victim had been shot or stabbed and said he thought the offender might still be on scene. But the officer who had called Dan really wasn't making much sense.

I was happy to learn that it was an indoor crime scene. It's always a good thing when it's an indoor crime scene. Chicago is known for its unpredictable weather and wind, hence the nickname the "Windy City." An indoor crime scene means you don't have to worry about rain, sleet, or snow—or evidence flying away. There are no spectators on the street, including annoying cameramen ready to take a photo of the victim lying lifeless in the street, without any concern for the family members who will undoubtedly see the photo pop up in their social media news feed. The media also seems to love the chance to get a photo of us detectives smiling and laughing, so they can show the world how mean and heartless the police are. When you're at a crime scene, you're often being recorded by news cameras the whole time. One little smile can be perceived as you being the insensitive detective who's cracking jokes while someone lies in the street after being brutally murdered.

But c'mon, you can hardly expect us to cry all day. Humor is a coping mechanism in my profession. We try to laugh every day so we don't cry every night. Most cops won't go to counseling for fear of saying something too honest and putting their job in jeopardy.

I tried counseling to deal with the aftermath of the demise of a relationship. Okay… I actually went to counseling once. The counselor thought my relationship was salvageable, so I knew he wasn't actually listening to me. I figured out this guy was better at Catholic marriage counseling and regardless of what we said to him, he was going to encourage working it out.

I headed out to the station to pick up a squad car. My regular partner John—they called us "Beauty and the Greek"—was running late. John was nicknamed "Greek Johnny Depp" in his old district because people thought he resembled Depp. I guess I could see the resemblance. John loved his ethnicity so much, it was all Greek all the time. Greek coffee, Greek salads, and only Greek-owned restaurants were his lunch choices. The only think that wasn't Greek was his wife.

So, instead of riding alone, I decided to jump in with Art and JC.

Art, one of the only multi-lingual Polish English detectives, was driving, so he immediately activated the lights and sirens in our unmarked squad car, a teal Ford Fusion. We seamlessly cut through the lanes, and traffic parted like the Red Sea.

It's hit or miss in Chicago with motorists' ability to pull to the right for sirens and lights. For some reason, just like when it rains and people forget how to drive, when a police car pops up behind them, people tend to abruptly stop or pull to the left. We need to get those old "Pull to the right for sirens and lights" bumper stickers back. But today was working out well for us, as far as traffic went.

I decided to call the other guys on our team: Greg Swiderek and Marco Garcia. Greg answered on the first ring and immediately relayed the info to Marco, who was apparently sitting next to him. It was evident that everyone was pleased with the fact that it was an indoor crime scene.

We arrived at the crime scene within minutes. The murder was actually located in an apartment in a mid-rise building just blocks away from my old condo. I had the luxury of living in a neighborhood on the city's sprawling lakefront, in a luxurious 650-square-foot condo that would have amazing lake views if I wasn't on the second floor. After I got married, I moved to the Northwest Side of the city with all of the other city workers. Uptown was a unique area; nonetheless, the neighborhood wasn't without its fair share of problems. There were a few criminal street gangs here and there and robberies occurred daily. However, it was nothing like the West Side of Chicago. But this wasn't Lincoln Park either. This was Uptown. And I was an Uptown girl. Siri, play "Uptown Girl" by Billy Joel.

A good homicide detective takes note of everything on the way to and upon arriving at a crime scene. That means we look, listen, smell, and feel everything around us. And instead of looking in front of us, we often look behind to see what happens as we drive away. In this case, the first thing I noticed was the fact that the forensic investigators' vehicle was still on scene, parked right in front. I knew that meant the victim's body was probably still on scene. This murder happened around 5:00 a.m., which was still part of the midnight shift. I'd gotten this call in the afternoon, before my shift started, because Sergeant Guzman thought I could get a head start on things. And in terms of crime scenes, this is exactly what you want. You want the victim's body left on scene and as close to the way it was found as possible. The most important piece of evidence in a homicide investigation is the body. The Chicago Fire Department has a big footprint, which often results in them destroying crime scenes before detectives even arrive on the scene.

There is a time-honored tradition of a playful rivalry and banter between cops and firefighters. They love to flex their muscles and use all of their fun equipment to break things. We always say they show up after the danger is gone, and then they get to pose shirtless for calendars while we do the real work. Never engage a fireman in a conversation about what they do every day unless you want an in-depth tutorial on how to properly use the Jaws of Life, a hydraulic device used to free people trapped inside a vehicle. That simple definition would then be followed by fifteen minutes of humble bragging about how many lives they've saved. I say this in an attempt at joking. Firemen love to talk about their jobs and will go into detail about the heat, the smoke, and the close calls they've encountered. Cops usually won't tell you a story until someone asks. Our stories don't often have happy endings and often, they start with someone else's tragedy.

At the end of the day, police and fire are actually on the same team and always back each other up. And the banter is mostly in good fun. Firefighters think cops sit in their cars all day, writing tickets. Cops think firemen spend their shifts sleeping and perfecting their favorite chili recipe. The truth is probably somewhere in the middle.

I was once in a terrible car accident on the way home from work as a new detective in 2007. It was Memorial Day. I was driving home after a midnight shift, wide awake and looking for an open coffee shop. "Straight home" was what one of the senior guys said to me as I walked out. When I think of that now, all I say to myself is "jinx." I'd baked cupcakes earlier in the day before work, a rare domestic victory in a life mostly filled with chaos, and had them sitting on the back seat in a box waiting for delivery to my then boyfriend. The streets were mostly empty, the city still asleep.

I was at the intersection waiting for the green light. I don't remember seeing the car, just a flash of movement and then the sound—the kind of sound you never forget. Someone had run the red light and hit me broadside, full force. The impact came out of nowhere, crushing metal and glass in a split second. My SUV folded like a soda can.

When everything stopped moving, I realized I was hanging upside down, still strapped into my seatbelt. My truck had flipped over and smashed into a pole. Cupcakes were everywhere—in my hair, smashed into the ceiling— and my gun had twisted into the loops of my pants. It was chaos, but strangely quiet inside that wreck. I remember thinking, *Is this it?*

Someone was talking to me from outside the vehicle. He was telling me I was going to be okay.

*Oh no!* I thought to myself. *He's doing the death talk that I've done so many times.* You tell people they're going to be okay, even when you know they're not.

The firemen had to pull me out through the windshield. They worked fast, talking to me the whole time, their calm voices cutting through the sirens and the smell of gasoline. I could feel shards of glass embedded in my scalp, blood trickling down my face, and pain radiating through my neck and back. Later, I would learn that I had ruptured discs in my back, but in that moment, I was just grateful to still be able to move. I remember looking at my hands and being shocked that I could move my fingers.

It's a miracle my neck wasn't broken. I'd seen tragedy a thousand times through my work, but that day, I felt it firsthand. I refused to drive through that intersection for years after the accident. So instead of reliving it, I just chose not to ever think about it. Moments like that show you how thin the line is between normal life and tragedy, a line I've walked my entire career. And now, standing in front of this Uptown building, that line was waiting for me again. A woman dead in her bed. And everything was about to unfold.

This woman on the bed, though battered and bloody, wasn't lingering. She was gone. Or at least that's what I believed. Maybe it's what I wanted to believe. I silently said a prayer for her.

After taking a look at the victim, it was time to do a cursory search of the crime scene in an attempt to identify any and all evidence. This apartment was lived in by a forty-ish single woman, so you can imagine the stuff in the home. Lots of shoes and clothes everywhere. Papers and bills and magazines and mail all over. The house wasn't dirty, but it was definitely messy. It was a bit reminiscent of the chaos I created when I was getting ready to go out on a Friday night. There were a few framed photos of the victim with various girlfriends and perhaps sisters or cousins. The photos must have been pretty old, because she looked very young in most of them. No pictures of any guys yet.

The dishes weren't done. Empty cups were on the table, counter, and dresser. Cigarette butts lay in an ashtray in the bedroom. A half-smoked marijuana blunt covered in shiny lip gloss sat on a windowsill. I didn't know about all of the new contraptions people used to get high, but I remembered the distinct smell of marijuana from high school. I also knew the distinct smell of bad weed or what they called skunk weed, the stuff a molecule away from being an actual weed. In high school, I never really hung around with people who used drugs. I think it's mostly because none of us could afford to do drugs. Back then, alcohol was the drug of choice. Real drugs were for the suburbanites.

I decided I needed to find her purse, so I looked around and found about five handbags. Each one was stuffed with receipts, sanitizer, random gift cards, mints, spare change, and lip gloss. But I still hadn't found the "real" purse. That's the one that her cell phone and wallet would be in. I would know when I found it, but I didn't expect to see any cash inside, and not because she'd been robbed. No one carried cash anymore, especially not women. Women used their credit cards and gift cards or cell phone apps for everything. I might expect to see a few dollars, but definitely no more than twenty bucks.

Back in the day, if you found a dead person with an empty wallet, it meant that robbery was likely the motive. Now it didn't mean a thing. I thought it would be more alarming to find large wads of cash than to have none at all. I wasn't completely eliminating the possibility that the victim had been robbed, just pointing out the obvious.

These days, the victim's cell phone held the key to everything, so I needed to find her phone. As I was looking around the apartment, I immediately noticed multiple windows located in the living room and dining room looking out onto Montrose Avenue. The curtains were wide open.

I walked up to the massive windows overlooking Montrose Avenue and let my eyes settle on the brown brick apartment building directly across the street. From this height, the distance between us felt nonexistent. It hit me almost immediately. I could see straight into the building. Every unit faced us like an open book. Not a single curtain. No blinds. No attempt at privacy. Just exposed windows stacked floor to floor.

The nosy neighbor in me kicked in automatically. Anyone in that building could have seen something. Lights, movement, shadows, sounds. Perhaps even murder. Potential witnesses hiding in plain sight. I made a mental note, already cataloging floors and angles, when something completely unrelated hijacked my attention.

On one of the exterior decks, framed perfectly by the window, there was a couple, completely naked, locked in each other, wrapped up in their own world. They moved with the confidence of people who either didn't care who was watching or assumed no one was. Or maybe they were freaks who hoped we were watching. Given the circumstances, it was surreal. Inside, we were processing the aftermath of a brutal crime. Outside, life was going on loud, reckless, and oblivious. Wow. I guessed nothing could kill their mood. I kind of wanted to commend them for that.

I paused what I was doing for a moment. Purely investigative, of course. I studied the scene the way I studied everything else: details, timing, and awareness. I was fairly certain they noticed me watching. A second later, I knew they had because we made direct eye contact. It was brief, almost defiant. They didn't stop. They didn't flinch. They just continued, as if daring the world to look away.

That's when the moment lost its novelty. The shock faded, the curiosity disappeared, and the scene became just another reminder of how disconnected reality could be. A terrible crime inside these walls. Indifference across the street. I turned back to my work, refocused, the image already filed away under things you don't forget but don't dwell on, either.

So, I went back to the shoe rack with all of the shoes that would never be worn again. That's when I noticed something peculiar. There was a pair of binoculars sitting on the window sill. This wasn't really an area where you could do much bird watching or sightseeing, so the binoculars struck me as being strange. So, as I sifted through the victim's personal belongings and read her mail and went through her drawers, I still didn't have a clear vision of who she was.

We have a thing called victimology. This basically is the way we look at a victim's habits and daily life to see if any factors in their lifestyle contributed to them becoming a victim. We're looking for things that could be considered high risk. That's drug use, promiscuity, illegal activity, etc. This can help us get information on how and why the victim ended up in this type of situation.

For me, nothing was standing out right now. This appeared to be a crime of passion, but this killer also wanted her dead, so it was way too soon to even try to guess what had actually happened here. Other than the small amount of marijuana in the house and some powder cocaine we found in her bedroom… this victim seemed to live a pretty low key life. I mean, from her credit card statements, she had a savings account with a few thousand dollars, a checking account with almost two thousand dollars in it, and a few small credit card bills. She had some utility bills and appeared to have her finances pretty much in order. She worked at a hair salon and did some volunteer work and back-to-school drives.

I decided to look at her bank statements again and didn't notice anything odd. No large deposits, no large withdrawals. It just looked like a regular working girl's life. I would have to figure out where her salon was located so we could stop by as soon as possible and try to find out a little more about her. I was still finding it odd that no one had shown up at her house to check on her. As I looked through the house, I saw a few greeting cards among the papers and junk in one of the junk drawers. I was getting a sense of how much this woman was loved and how much she loved life.

Crime scene investigators, or forensic investigators, which is what we call them in Chicago, would swab everything for DNA or blood evidence and collect anything that might be physical evidence. A good forensic investigator will bend over backward for you. If you get a bad one, they'll still bend over backward but complain the whole time about how overworked they are. Forensic investigators and evidence technicians are overworked. They go from job to job without pause.

Today, as luck would have it, we got a good one. We got Dave Ryan. This six-foot-four gentle giant worked more overtime than anyone in the city, probably in the world. His memory was impeccable. Dave could recall every bit of evidence from crime scenes even years after they happened… in a cute *Rain Man* sort of way. Dave always reminded me of my youngest sister's late father Mike. They looked so much alike they could have been brothers. I'd shown Dave photos of Mike, and even he agreed there was a striking resemblance.

Thank God it was Dave. There were so many items here it was hard to discern what was evidence and what wasn't. The site immediately reminded me of the Amanda Knox story and the way the investigators had botched that crime scene. What ensued after that was chaos, to say the least.

Knox was the American girl living in Italy who was accused of murdering her roommate during an alleged sexcapade gone wrong in 2007. The case was all over the news for years. Sloppy evidence handling included a bra clasp that sat on the floor for more than six weeks before it was collected. Crime scene photos show that it had been moved from its original location before it was recovered. As a seasoned detective, I'm usually skeptical when high profile suspects proclaim their innocence. Usually the evidence paints a different story. But in the case of Amanda Knox, I actually believed she was mostly telling the truth. And when I say mostly, I mean there's no mistake; no one tells the truth, the full truth, and nothing but the truth. Everyone lies for different reasons. Our job is just to figure out which parts are lies and why they're lying about it. Sometimes it's not malicious. Sometimes people lie because they're embarrassed to tell you the truth about something. Sometimes people lie out of habit.

Crime scene destruction, though... that wasn't going to happen here, not with Dave and definitely not with me. Too bad there weren't more Daves on the job. He really was one of a kind, the guy who would rake through the grass for hours in an effort to find the one little bullet fragment you knew was there, but no one else could see. He was the guy who would take the whole futon mattress from a crime scene, not just a slice of the fabric, if there was even the remote possibility that the offender left his DNA on it. Dave was truly the best.

Today, this crime scene was mine and my partner John's. No idea what in the world made this guy decide to go into law enforcement, but he's the real deal. John's one of those people who seems like an enigma. He's so different from most folks who choose this line of work. He's got a presence about him, calm and steady, no matter the situation, but I've always thought he's got a secret side to him that nobody quite understands.

The funny thing is, John never planned on becoming a cop in the first place. When he started, he lied to his whole family about what he was doing. He took the police exam and did well, but his plan was to drop out before anything got serious. He started the whole process, thinking there would be a moment when he could just back out. But somehow, he kept pushing through. Finally, when the offer came for him to join the academy, things got real and he still hadn't told anyone.

His mom had her heart set on John working a "real" job. She'd always dreamed of him becoming something successful, and for her, that meant a life in business. She wanted him to be a stock boy, or so she said in her adorable Greek accent, her English a bit broken around the edges. Turns out, she meant "stock broker," but her loose translation always cracked us up. For years, John got the brunt of our jokes about being a stock boy. We all teased him, telling him that maybe, just maybe, he was meant to stand on the floors of some corporate high-rise, counting inventory and wearing a suit, not running around crime scenes. But the truth was, law enforcement had always been in his blood, even if he didn't know it at the time. Well, that and real estate. John also does real estate on the side, like a lot of cops.

John is the guy who is always in a good mood. He's also always late for work, but he makes up for it by staying long after we've all gone home. John's clocks are also different from ours. Our clock says 5:55 p.m. To John, that's 5:00 p.m. on the dot. Greeks get their own Easter too.

As soon as the Greek Church was over, John would be waltzing through the door with theories on who committed this murder. But until then, I would handle it.

True to form, John walked in just as Dave was taking video and photographs of the crime scene. We took a walk and talked through the scene with the A-Team. Dave immediately took multiple swabs of the blood near the entrance in the foyer of the apartment. All of this blood couldn't come from one person, right? The killer's DNA was going to be there somewhere. Or at least that's what I was hoping for. The next step was to head to the bedroom, where the victim lay in her bed. It was hard to miss the abrasion on the victim's head. Upon closer inspection, it appeared to be a gunshot wound. It was definitely an entrance wound.

Entrance wounds are neat and round and often symmetrical. Exit wounds are jagged and ugly.

Next up was my least favorite part: flipping over the body. The point of this is to look for additional evidence and wounds. Since this was an especially bloody crime scene, the doubled-up purple latex gloves I was wearing might prove to be insufficient. I was sure my black pants, gray shirt, and black leather jacket were already soiled with blood. But these clothes had seen it before. My Marshalls department store clearance comfort pumps would no doubt have to be thrown out after this one. The blood was probably seeping into the rubber heels even with the surgical footsies I was wearing. Thank God I only paid thirty bucks for them.

I asked Dave and Detective Greg to flip the victim over while I looked and wrote notes. A dead body really is dead weight. It's a struggle to flip over even a small girl like this victim. It's even worse when rigor mortis sets in and they become stiff. That's why there's a technique to it, and it's nothing they teach you in detective school. You learn it by trial and error after soiling many outfits, ruining bulletproof vest covers, and getting blood flicked in your face, mouth, and eyes. All part of the glamorous job. Greg had done this many times before, so I figured he should do it.

Looking around the apartment, we now had to decide what was evidence and what was just "stuff." This wasn't Mayberry, where there was one murder a year and unlimited resources. This was Chicago. So, what I normally did on any type of crime scene was collect everything that might possibly be evidence and conduct immediate testing on what I knew was evidence. The rest could always be tested later. I'd learned not to leave anything behind because once it was gone, it was gone forever.

I guess that saying goes for most things in life.

As I randomly ran through the items I believed would be the most important evidence, I silently prayed I wasn't missing anything. The evidence included cigarette butts, a half-smoked blunt, possible DNA on the drinking glasses left around, the bills on the counter, and the sheets on the bed. There was a shattered .38 revolver on the floor and a million knives in the kitchen drawers and in the sink. I kept thinking I might be missing something. Something obvious.

"Okay, Michele," I said to myself, "one last look around." The little voice in my head seemed to agree with me. I was missing something, but I wouldn't find it until later.

As usual, the processing of this crime scene was taking hours upon hours, with no break in sight. Finally, the crime scene processing was done. It was almost time to go eat. I was so hungry I thought about eating a few of the crackers I'd found in the pantry. I thought about it, but decided that was probably a bad idea.

At this moment, my thought process was interrupted by the loud noises coming from my stomach. It was growling so loudly I was pretty sure people around me could hear it. I realized I was famished. I wished I had a granola bar or something in my bag. I usually carried something around with me, but I'd been so busy lately I hadn't made it to the grocery store in probably weeks. I searched my pockets and found a crushed up stick of gum in the bottom of the pocket of my bulletproof vest. I scraped most of the foil wrapper off and popped it in my mouth. That should hold me over for a bit.

I was surprised no neighbors had come by to ask about Yolanda or give us any information. Normally, this was the point where the nosy neighbors came over to see what was going on. That set off a red flag for me. Didn't anyone care about Yolanda? Shouldn't they be worried about the killer on the loose? I was sure the news about her death had already spread like wildfire. Or were they avoiding us?

I was guessing the canvass detectives from midnights didn't come up with any witnesses because I hadn't heard from them since we arrived on scene. Oh well, we would definitely come back here and go door to door to talk to everyone in the building. Someone had to know something. Now, the trick was to figure out who, and then to get the details out of them.

The midnight detectives located a cell phone near Yolanda's body. From what I could tell, it looked like it belonged to her. Thankfully, it was an iPhone and I had a charger, so I would be able to charge it up so the phone didn't shut off, which would make it harder to forensically examine later. I walked over to the bathroom again and noticed that there was urine in the toilet. Aside from being grossed out, I was fairly certain that this sample was left by one of the police officers on scene because I definitely didn't notice it before. Guys never see a problem with peeing inside a murder victim's bathroom. Not me. I'm a lady. So, I hold it all night until I make it to our lunch location. However, it's a little known fact that urine is almost void of any DNA and in terms of evidentiary value, it really has almost none unless someone had a raging urinary tract infection and blood is present. Even that is near impossible to test with our laboratories. I decided not to spend any more time thinking about the officer who couldn't have the decency to walk outside to pee. Finally, the crime scene processing was done. We still had to make official family notification to Yolanda's next of kin. The midnight detectives talked to a couple of people, including her son Qaw'mane, but he was too distraught to help.

Hopefully, one of her family members or even a close friend would call her. I would keep her phone on me until that happened. I decided to stick around and wait for the body removal service, otherwise known as the "body snatchers," to remove the victim's body. Whenever you think your job sucks, think about these guys. They go from crime scene to crime scene, tagging and bagging people who died in ways you cannot imagine.

The phone number for the medical examiner's office is 666-0200. I'm not kidding. Every time I dial it, I think the same thing: whoever assigned that number had a dark sense of humor, or no sense at all.

It's one of those details you don't forget once you learn it and, unfortunately, it's a detail I have to pass along far too often. I always cringe when the moment comes, when I have to say it out loud to family members who are already shattered, already hanging on by a thread. I'll give the number slowly, clearly, trying to keep my voice steady, and then it happens every single time. "Wait… what?"

They look at me like I've just made a cruel mistake. Like I'm messing with them. Like there's no way the office responsible for their loved one could possibly have a phone number that starts with *that*. I can almost see the thought cross their face. *Is this some kind of joke?*

I rush to reassure them. "I know," I say. "It really is the number." Sometimes, I even repeat it, as if repetition will make it less horrifying. It never does. There's something especially brutal about that moment. As if death itself hasn't already taken enough, now it's stamped with a number straight out of a bad horror movie. It feels unnecessary, cruel in a bureaucratic way. Another reminder that once someone crosses into that world, even the smallest details lose their humanity. I hate giving that number out. Not because I forget it, but because I can't.

The body snatchers arrived and put on their white hazmat suits. They always look like they're ready to clean up a nuclear spill. Some of them opt to wear only part of the suit, and others put on every piece of equipment and look like the original Ghostbusters. Either way, they aren't getting paid enough. Sometimes, I wish I could tip them to show my appreciation for a job well done, but that probably wouldn't go over well. I think they could supplement their income with a little tip jar. They definitely deserve it more than the barista who makes my Americano at the coffee shop. Lately, it seems like everyone asks for tips for doing their job. These guys should get a little tip when they get to an especially messy crime scene or when they arrive on scene within thirty minutes like Domino's Pizza.

We had two body snatchers today. I made small talk with them, and they told me this was their fifth body of the day.

The body snatchers only come when the victim becomes a medical examiner's case. That's usually murder, suicide, a drug overdose, or really anything that isn't your run of the mill natural death. These guys only take the body to the county morgue, which in Chicago is called the Cook County Medical Examiner's Office.

In other cases, where someone dies and it's not suspicious, the deceased's body is released to the family, and they provide their own transport to the funeral home. Anytime I ask myself who would take this job—I mean, who the fuck wants to deal with dead people day in and day out?—I have to remind myself of what I do for a living and that people must say the same thing about me.

Yolanda was finally hastily placed in a thick, black plastic zip-up body bag and rolled onto an aluminum gurney. She was then rolled away toward the elevator. I could hear that one of the wheels needed to be oiled because it squeaked loudly as they rolled her away. These guys must have been working together for a while, because I realized they didn't say one word to each other. They got in and out pretty quickly too. It was kind of like the perfectly choreographed dance. Neither of them stepped on the other's toes and no one's foot got rolled over by the wheels on the gurney. But they definitely weren't best friends. I immediately wondered if they get paid by the body. Now, that's an incentive that would improve productivity.

The victim was wheeled out of the apartment and onto the elevator. Luckily, they didn't have to make that trip on the stairs. The bag was thick enough so it wouldn't leak, but the body was getting pretty stiff, so maneuvering her down even one flight of stairs would have been really tough. When I first went on the job, we had to transport our own dead bodies. This meant bagging them and putting them in the back of the police wagon any way we could. We started getting hazmat pay, and then the department decided to do away with it and simply outsource it. I'm sure it saved them money and cut down on accidents and injuries from police officers trying to drag a dead body into a wagon.

One of the first dead bodies I handled in Area Three came from an anonymous 311 non-emergency call. A woman had dialed in, claiming that her friend had a dead body in the closet in his apartment, and that he was trying to find someone to pay to get rid of it or help him dump it in Lake Michigan. She didn't offer much more information, no details about the body, no explanation of how the person had died. For whatever reason, instead of the usual patrol officers, they somehow managed to get a hold of the Detective Division. Sergeant Bob Elmore, one of my sergeants, asked me to accompany him to the suspect's house. It was just a few blocks away from the station, and we both figured it was probably a prank call, something ridiculous that wasn't worth much of our time.

We knocked on the door, and a middle-aged White guy with shaggy blond hair answered. He didn't seem rattled, but there was something off about him, like he wasn't fully processing what was happening.

I didn't waste time with pleasantries. I just said, "Hello, my name is Detective Michele Wood. Someone called and said you had a dead body in a closet in your house."

He just stared at me, his face a blank canvas. There was no panic, no confusion, just... nothing.

I pressed him again. "So, do you have a dead body in your house?

"No," he said flatly, as if offering a simple denial.

I looked at him, searching his eyes for a sign, then asked, "Are you sure?"

He hesitated for a moment, his gaze shifting, before finally saying, "Okay, she's right over there." He pointed toward the back of the apartment, like it was nothing.

We immediately did a protective pat-down and asked him if anyone else was inside. He told us he was alone. I radioed for backup, just in case. We cleared the house to make sure it was empty. Then he led us down the narrow hallway to a closet in the back of the apartment. Inside, wrapped tightly in a SpongeBob SquarePants blanket and duct-taped to a dolly on wheels, was what looked like a body.

The weight of the moment hit me in waves. We later learned the woman had died from what appeared to be a drug overdose. This guy, for whatever reason, had freaked out and decided to dispose of her himself instead of calling 911. He thought he could get away with it. But obviously, he was wrong.

Without hesitation, we took him into custody, but the real work was just beginning. We needed to get the body to the morgue. Back then, we didn't have the luxury of body snatchers to handle this sort of thing, so we had to make do with the wagon. John and I started wheeling the dolly toward the vehicle. The wheels squeaked under the weight and then, naturally, a tire went flat. The body shifted, and one of the victim's legs slipped out from the tightly wrapped blanket, a foot covered in a dingy white sneaker exposed for the world to see.

And of course, as we struggled to move the dolly, the neighbors in the Roscoe Village neighborhood gathered in front of their homes, their faces pressed up against their windows, watching the whole spectacle unfold. I couldn't help but feel the sting of their eyes, the whispers I could practically hear.

To top it all off, I was wearing my cutest pair of black pumps that day. This particular pair were ones I would normally save for court. They weren't special anymore. They were now soiled in human remains, caked in a reminder of the reality of the day.

So obviously, I have a special appreciation for the body snatchers and the work they do.

Yolanda was loaded into the transport van without any problems like the ones I'd experienced. She was on the way to the medical examiner's office. Then tomorrow morning at the crack of dawn, a medical examiner would conduct an autopsy. Depending on how late we stayed at work, I would decide if I attended the autopsy or simply made a phone call down to the police office at the morgue to get the results. At this point, we had a suspicion about how she'd died, but it's always a good idea to attend the autopsy in case you have questions or want additional testing. We also suspected that the cause of death determination would be "pending tox," which meant the victim's bodily fluids and tissues would be sent out for a postmortem toxicology exam. They would detect and measure levels of drugs, and this included prescription drugs, some over the counter, the street variety and, of course, poison. The decision could take weeks or even months.

Yolanda's autopsy would be interesting because of the fact that she'd suffered from two different injuries which could have been fatal in their own right. So, we would like to know which injury came first. That was definitely a question that only the medical examiner could answer… Well, I guess so could Yolanda's boyfriend Curtis.

After speaking to Curtis and having him explain his version of the story for the umpteenth time, he agreed to take a lie detector test. He said he would do whatever it took to find who killed the love of his life. Greg and Marco volunteered to drive him to the lie box technician on the South Side. I had too much else to do to on this case right now, so I couldn't sit there for hours. Marco and Greg had their own cases, but they decided to help me out. Greg gave me a few smart comments about arresting Curtis after he failed the test. He was really doing me a favor anyway, giving me time to get back to figuring out what had happened.

Cops and their egos! Everyone wants to be the first arresting officer. There can be ten names on the report, but everyone cares about the name in Box One.

"Sure," I told Greg, "if you can prove he did it."

So, I was all that was left. Everyone else took off. The victim was gone and it was eerily silent. The air was thick and kind of hot and stale. The blood in the hallway was starting to smell like rotting flesh. I decided to open the windows a bit to get some fresh air. One thing Chicago Police aren't in charge of is post crime scene cleaning. I'm guessing there are lots of companies that do that. But we don't provide recommendations.

We made the decision not to release the crime scene just yet. Normally, once I leave the crime scene, there's no reason to return. But today, I decided to allow myself some time to think about it. If I happened to uncover some information later, I may have to come back to look for some evidence. Once we released the apartment to the building management company, the family members would show up and take anything valuable and then, inevitably, everything else would get thrown away. Who knew what I may need from here later. There was no rush to release the apartment just yet anyway. Not at this point.

All that was left were the thoughts racing in my mind. *What happened here?* I had to figure it out. No doubt I wouldn't be sleeping for the next few days. Insomnia and sleepwalking... another perk of my job no one told me about. I was never a great sleeper. As a kid, I would sleepwalk when I was stressed out. I seemed to have kept this habit or ailment with me through my whole life. It's nothing new to me because my little sister sleepwalks too, and so did my mom. It's obviously genetic. It can be comical at times, with friends at a sleepover or with a new boyfriend. But it's always something that has given me anxiety and even embarrassment. I've had many friends and a couple boyfriends who have been afraid and/or intrigued by the fact that I sleepwalk. When my mind races, I can't just shut it off. I've solved many murders while lying awake, unable to sleep. That's usually when I have that *Aha!* moment.

Another one of the hazards of this job is if you do too much without giving yourself a break, you'll start seeing everything when you close your eyes. That's where compartmentalizing becomes a good thing. I guess normal people aren't supposed to do this, but sometimes believing is better than real life.

We finally decided to get out of the apartment. We would be back later or maybe tomorrow. I needed to talk to these neighbors. All of this blood and no one heard anything? Unbelievable. I needed to take another look around the apartment too, not necessarily for evidence. I was looking for something that I couldn't quite put my finger on. It was finally time to get out of this place and go eat. Thank God! I was starting to go stir crazy. The other members of my team had let me know they would be headed to the twenty-four-hour Golden Nugget diner located near our station for lunch.

It doesn't matter if it's morning, noon, or night, it's still called lunch. For detectives who work the night shift—AKA, the third watch—you usually try to go to lunch immediately after roll call. You never know where the night might take you. A hungry detective isn't an efficient detective. And a drunk is better than no detective. The latter part is a story for another time.

# CHAPTER 6

# WE HAVE SOME BAD NEWS FOR YOU

Even though Curtis agreed to be strapped up to the lie detector and Yolanda's body was off to the morgue, this case was nowhere near wrapped. In homicide, interviews are your lifeline. But the interviews that really matter are the ones that come from the family. They know the patterns, the secrets… including the break ups and the make ups. In Yolanda's case, the sister was the closest thread we had left to pull. We were hoping she had some kind of information that could help us move this case forward.

John and I decided to take one more walk through Yolanda's apartment after lunch and put a coroner's seal on the door. The coroner's seal meant it was illegal for anyone other than the authorized law enforcement personnel to open the door or enter the crime scene. The seal was actually a sticky piece of paper that held about as much weight as the warning label on a mattress. But at least it was something. So, we locked the door and headed off to lunch before deciding our next move, which was to hit the ground and talk to some people.

We decided that we should talk to Yolanda's sister Tiffany again as soon as possible. It looked like she lived right outside of Chicago in a western suburb. That's always a fun little road trip when you're a city detective running on fumes. And normally, pulling up to a relative's home after a homicide puts us right into that category of things we absolutely hate doing: next of kin notifications. Those are the moments where your stomach tightens, because you never know what's on the other side of that door. People react in ways you could write an entire psychology textbook about. I've seen everything from a family member who seemed as emotionally invested as someone watching a rerun on the Game Show Network, to someone who dropped so fast I honestly thought I was going to have to start CPR right on their welcome mat.

But in this case, we weren't going to knock on the door and drop the bomb for the first time. The detectives who had handled the initial response had already notified Yolanda's sister. She already knew her sister was gone. She knew as much as they could tell her. She knew her sister had been murdered. So technically, I wasn't walking up to her house with that awful burden on my shoulders. But just because the notification had already been done didn't mean the air was any lighter. The grief would still be there. The shock would still be there. And when you walk into a home after a brutal murder, you still brace yourself to absorb whatever emotion hits you. It's never really "over." You just don't have to say the words.

Our job now was to get an in-depth interview with her, to gather whatever she knew—history, arguments, patterns, fears, friends, exes, anything that might point us in a direction. And I was told the sisters were extremely close. That's both a blessing and a curse in homicide work. Close meant she might know something. Close also meant her grief might be a tidal wave we would have to wade through before we could even form a question.

We tried calling her a couple times on the cell phone number she'd provided to the other detectives. She didn't answer. Generally, I'm a big believer in the sneak attack. I don't like announcing myself unless I absolutely have to.

When people know the police are coming, they rehearse, they call their cousin who knows a cousin who has a friend who once talked to an attorney, and suddenly everyone has a brand-new version of the truth. People lie and hide things for reasons that would baffle God Himself. But when you show up unannounced, you get the raw version—raw house, raw face, raw emotions. And I love a good look around someone's home. You can learn more from someone's fridge, shoes by the door, mail piled up on the counter, and the state of their bathroom than you'll get from an hour-long interview. I'm nosy, but there's a purpose for it. As we drove toward her house in the nearby suburbs, John and I sat in complete silence. Partly because we were exhausted, and partly because if we spoke to each other any more that night, one of us would snap. It's not natural to spend this much time with one person. Even married couples take breaks from each other with errands or a long shower or zoning out watching TV. Detectives? We're stuck in a car together all day, all night, and then we get told to "just keep working." I'm sure we were both sick of the sound of each other's breathing.

It was shaping up to be one of those nights where every time you think you can finally go home, something else gets tacked on. Detective Groundhog Day. The only saving grace was music. And 2012… God, what a year for music. We didn't appreciate it until later. But at the time, it was the only thing keeping us from killing each other. Years later, we would still bring up how good those songs were, like old people reminiscing about the Golden Age of Radio.

As we got closer, I mentally rehearsed what I might say to Tiffany. Even though we weren't making the notification, we still had to be mindful walking into a grieving person's home. And it reminded me of the way we normally deliver death notifications. People assume we soften it. They picture us using gentle euphemisms like, "Your loved one has gone to a better place." But no… because then they ask, "Oh?

Where?" And let me tell you, nothing kills the moment faster than realizing you now have to explain the logistics of heaven to someone whose life just imploded.

No, in homicide we do it like ripping off a Band-Aid: "Your sister Yolanda was shot and she's dead." Brutal, but necessary. Clear. No room for interpretation. We don't do poetry; we do facts. But today, those words weren't mine to say. Someone else already had to carry that weight. Tonight, we were here for answers, though I already suspected we weren't going to get any meaningful ones out of her, not while the loss was this fresh.

We pulled onto her tree-lined suburban street. It was so dark I had to squint to see the house numbers. Streetlights were doing their best, but that early-morning, half-dead detective brain wasn't compatible with dim lighting. We spotted her house. It was a neat little brick ranch with updated picture windows and fresh tuck pointing. Lights on inside, a TV flickering in the living room. It looked warm, lived-in, and normal. I always get hit with a weird feeling on scenes like this. A home can feel so safe from the outside while someone inside is going through the worst moment of their life.

We swung around back to make sure nothing strange was happening. Old habits. If you work homicides long enough, you learn that the back door is where the secrets live. The yard was tidy but scattered with toys, bright play sets, little shoes, and a kiddie pool flipped on its side and filled with old leaves. The blinds on the back windows were closed, and there were no lights on. Good. The kids were probably asleep.

We drove back to the front and parked a few houses down. Walked up, knocked, and even shone a flashlight through the side window. Nothing. No movement, no shadow, no peeking through blinds. At that point, exhaustion trumped optimism. We tried. She wasn't answering. And honestly?

I was done for the day. Emotionally, mentally, physically done. John and the team felt the same. We'd hit our limit.

It was our "Friday," which in the detective world meant it was actually Tuesday, but we were off the next two days. Close enough. They wanted to go have a drink, and though I usually avoid cop bars like the plague, tonight I needed something to take the edge off. My pugs weren't going to scold me for coming home late.

When I finally got home, I was over-tired, but I tossed and turned in the middle of the night and suddenly, I looked up to find a masked man standing over my bed. I couldn't see his face in the dark. *Fuck, he's here. He finally found me.*

I remembered that my gun was under my bed. Thank God. But then I grabbed for my gun and he reached for it at the same time, and I was finally able to get a firm grip on it and slowly pulled the trigger. But nothing happened. I was in a complete panic now and I realized my gun wasn't working. This was how I would die.

I immediately woke up in a cold sweat and realized I'd been dreaming again.

I have this dream all the time. Over the years, I've had the same few recurring nightmares that happen over and over. It's worse when I'm stressed out or sleep deprived. I don't think I've ever met a cop who hasn't had the same dream about firing their gun and nothing happening or the bullet traveling slowly—or worse, the bullet hitting the bad guy and nothing happens. If you look it up, there's a million different reasons why it occurs, but basically it's caused by stress.

This isn't a job for everyone. It's not natural to work twenty-four hours straight. It's not natural to deal with such sadness and despair, not to mention the danger we face every single day. I used to be a carefree, easygoing gal. Now, I rarely leave the house without my gun. I never want to be the one who wasn't prepared. I don't want to be the next victim.

# CHAPTER 7

# WALKING CONTRADICTION

People always told me they could hear me before they saw me. The click of my heels on the station floor had its own rhythm… sharp, steady, unapologetic. I didn't tiptoe anywhere. Maybe it was my shoes, maybe it was the way I walked, or maybe it was just the pace of my life back then: fast, focused, constantly in motion. Either way, my presence usually announced itself before I even rounded a corner. And honestly? I didn't mind. Being one of the only women in Homicide, the sound of those heels felt like my own little calling card. It said "I belong here"—without me ever having to raise my voice.

Greg, one of the guys on my team, used to imitate my hallway walk. He would stomp dramatically and throw his shoulders back like a cartoon version of me. The whole floor would crack up. And I would too, because I wasn't offended. I knew exactly what he was portraying. I walked hard because I had to. In a room full of men, your stride becomes another tool in your belt. Sometimes it speaks for you before you get a chance to say a word.

Chicago is a place where characters appear out of nowhere, and the police department is no different. You meet every kind of person, from the neighbor with a front-porch law degree to celebrities who drift in and out of the city like smoke. And every now and then, one of those characters ends up at the center of your next case.

It was a year before the big shake-up, summer of 2011, and we were still taking cases as they came in. Sometimes it was a death investigation, other times it was a shooting. On this particular day, one of the other detectives, Luke, whom we referred to as Dr. Death because he only handled death investigations, called me one afternoon and said, "Michele, I've got a DOA at a downtown hotel, looks like a big deal. Can you meet me at the scene?" The tone in his voice told me right away that it wasn't just another overdose.

By the time I got there, the whole scene had a different kind of energy. One of the luxury hotels downtown, white marble lobby, soft jazz, and a doorman who looked like he wanted to melt into the wallpaper. Upstairs, everyone was gathered around the deceased man: middle-aged White male lying face down on the bed, cold and stiff, long gone before anyone realized something was wrong. He had spiky, reddish-brown hair and a goatee that made him look just enough like actor Danny Bonaduce from the '70s *The Partridge Family* sitcom to make me hope, for everyone's sake, that it wasn't actually Danny Bonaduce.

The victim still had the tan lines from a wedding ring and a watch, but no jewelry in sight. His room was a nice one near the Magnificent Mile, which told me he wasn't a local. He looked like an out-of-towner who had ended up in the wrong situation, in the wrong city, at exactly the wrong time.

There's a meme that says, "Come to Chicago for the pizza, stay because you got murdered." Dark humor, but anyone who works here knows the sentiment didn't come out of nowhere. For this poor man, it felt uncomfortably close to the truth.

His suitcase sat neatly in the corner. The luggage tag listed only "Los Angeles, CA" and a phone number. No address. Great. I've never understood why people take the time to fill out half a tag. It's like handing me a puzzle with three pieces missing.

The room was unusually tidy. Minibar wiped out. Either he had an appetite, or someone had helped themselves after killing him. No wallet. No watch. No wedding ring. Robbery was looking likely. We didn't know his name yet, so I hoped he'd checked in under his real identity and that the hotel had followed protocol and scanned his ID. Otherwise, it was about to be a long night.

Somewhere in California, someone was going about their evening completely unaware that their world had already changed. That part never got easier. The tears aren't for the dead. They're for the people left behind who have to figure out their new "normal."

I walked the hallway, knocked on hotel room doors. Nobody answered. That didn't mean no one saw anything. Between the surveillance cameras and the guest list, we would piece something together. It always started messy before it started making sense.

We were high enough that nobody was scaling the building, not unless the perp was a *Mission Impossible* stuntman. The room door had been touched by half of the hotel staff already, but I propped it open for forensics anyway. Sometimes luck shows up in the strangest ways.

Downstairs, hotel security met me after I talked to the front desk, a young woman named Rachel with a British accent and perfect eyeliner. Security in these hotels is usually made up of people who want to get into law enforcement, so they're eager to help. But right then, I had a dead man upstairs.

By 9:00 p.m., I still didn't have the guest list. Management was gone. The CPD Video Retrieval Unit was tied up with a police shooting. If you ever want to see true chaos, show up at one of those. It's a full circus. This means news trucks, neighbors, lights, sirens, everyone trying to narrate what happened.

Back in the lobby, I noticed a group of glamorous, barely dressed women avoiding eye contact. The universal rule: if I don't see you, you don't see me. Not corporate types. Chicago still has districts running enforcement cars for prostitution, relics from decades ago when early-morning joggers were tired of running into the "hoe stroll." Chicago policing has its strange traditions.

Hours later, we finally got a name: Jack O'Connell. And he wasn't just any guest. He was a big-time Hollywood music producer in town for the Air and Water Show. Bigger than we expected, the kind of case the media would pounce on. My priority became getting someone to his family before a reporter or hashtag beat us to it.

Then the surveillance video started filling in the blanks. Luke showed me footage of the victim entering the hotel carrying a plastic Walgreens bag.

"What's in the bag?" I asked. Turns out it was Jolly Ranchers, Slim Jims, and aluminum foil. People with vices always have their quirks. Once I saw the aluminum foil, I immediately knew where this was going.

The medical examiner performed the autopsy the next day and ruled it "pending police investigation and toxicology exam." Later, I learned and confirmed the cause of death: heroin overdose. At first glance, you might think he'd been beaten. The decomposition may have been accelerated by the warm hotel room. Now the plan was simple: find "Sexy Ebony."

Summertime Chicago never slows down. Crime is our business, and business was booming that August. We started trying to identify and locate her. The case stalled. Leads dried up. People stopped answering phones. Chicago moved on, like it always does. But a couple weeks later, we finally figured out who she was and brought her in for questioning.

Once she was inside and settled, she opened up. Not just a little, either. She gave us the whole story. She told us where to find her accomplice... another working girl. We brought everyone in, got videotaped statements from everyone. It helped us lay out the chain of events.

It turned out O'Connell had gone on Backpage classifieds, Craigslist's seedier cousin, to find drugs. Not sex, drugs. Specifically cocaine. Powder cocaine, not crack. He figured a prostitute would have connections. He was on some kind of Hollywood fad diet and was in the process of breaking a "fast" of sorts.

The woman he'd found called herself Sexy Ebony. She showed up at the hotel, he told her what he wanted, and she made a call to her friend. But powder coke isn't easy to find on the West Side of Chicago. Crack and heroin run the streets there. Her friend couldn't get coke but could get white powder heroin, close enough to fool an outsider.

Sexy Ebony returned and handed the heroin over, calling it "good stuff." O'Connell snorted three bags, thinking it was coke, while she attempted to give him an erotic massage that he wasn't interested in. Sometime later, when he fell unconscious, she decided to cut her losses and leave. Before leaving, she stole jewelry, cash, and his wedding ring. At some point during the night, she'd somehow gotten him to go to the ATM a few times to get more cash. She left him face down in the hotel bed, not realizing—or maybe not caring—that he was slipping into cardiac arrest.

We told her everything, except one truth: the man she'd duped into taking too many of the wrong drugs had died. There's a moment I'll never forget. I asked, "What do you think happens if someone snorts three or four bags of heroin?" She looked me dead in the eyes and said, genuinely confused, "Shit. I don't know… they die?" She wasn't being sarcastic. She truly didn't know.

We put the pieces of the puzzle together and learned that hotel staff had found him cold the next morning after friends reported he never showed up for lunch. When we pulled the surveillance footage, it tied the whole thing together: Sexy Ebony walking confidently in, scantily clad, heels clicking, carrying a designer bag that was either fake or probably wasn't hers. Hours later, she walked out again, looking like she was in a rush, maybe realizing things had gone south.

This was before catfishing became mainstream, but she definitely catfished him. The girl in the Backpage ad wasn't her. Not even close. Bait and switch. I'm sure he was perplexed, expecting Sexy Ebony and instead getting someone who looked like she'd crawled out of a sewer.

After wrapping the interviews, we presented the case to the State's Attorney's Office. Everything was tight. We had statements, timelines, admissions. Still, they refused to charge the woman or her shady friend in connection with Jack O'Connell's death. I was upset. We all were. But they said a jury would never convict on those facts.

These are the moments that stick with you as a detective: you can do everything right, build the case brick by brick, and still watch justice slip through your fingers.

# CHAPTER 8

## CONNER'S ANGELS

When I was a rookie, I patrolled the Shakespeare District, Logan Square's own tangle of corner stores, CTA "L" tracks, and stoops that had been my back yard long before it was my beat. Walking those streets felt like coming home in uniform: familiar storefronts, old neighborhood rhythms, the way the light hit the brick in late afternoon. It didn't take long to remember the neighborhood's unspoken language. The international sign of disrespect when an officer pulls someone over? A loud, theatrical loogie spat out upon the officer's approach. I saw it time and again on traffic stops with gang members; it was ritual, contempt made physical. Every time, a small, ridiculous wish flared up in me to beat them to it, to spit first, and then my own reflex would win: I was too much of a lady for that kind of petty performance. So I stood there, uniform crisp, breathing slow, letting the moment live in my mind.

This is the place where I started my career and in 2001, I got paired up with my first field training officer, William, AKA Billy Conners. We were assigned beat 1411 on the third watch, working 3:00 p.m. to 11:00 p.m. Billy was a tall, stern salt-and-pepper-haired man with a tough disposition and a 1980s Tom Selleck mustache, with a love for menthol cigarettes and Wild Turkey and a heart of gold. Bill could be a muse for any TV police procedural show creator.

I remember the day I met Billy. He put out his hand to shake mine and looked me up and down—not in a creepy way, but in a way like he was sizing me up and was already disappointed by what he saw. His expression said, "Great, they stuck me with her."

I didn't care. I was used to it. I wasn't going to let one judgmental stare get to me.

Billy carried himself like someone who had seen it all and had zero patience for bullshit. But I could see under his gruff demeanor there was a quiet curiosity. I knew I would prove him wrong. I kept my tone respectful and answers short and tried to absorb every single thing he told me. I think after our first job together, he knew I was going to be one of the good ones. "You're okay, kid," he would later tell me.

He always said we weren't speeding to any call unless a police officer was calling for help. A 10-1 is what we call that. A 10-1 means an officer is in distress. And no, that didn't mean that regular calls weren't worthy of a rapid response; it just meant that getting there safely was of utmost importance. We couldn't help people if we didn't get there in one piece. Every time you blow through a red light or a stop sign, you're taking a risk. No matter how many times you flash your lights or blast your siren, someone will inevitably not be paying attention. Bill knew what he was talking about. He'd been working his beat on the north side of the district for twenty-five years when I met him. That meant he knew every single customer, as he would call them. I'm sure Bill wasn't enthused to work with me because all he knew about me was that I was a former Hooters Girl and flight attendant who lived in the district.

Did I forget to mention that I also lived on beat 1411? Well, yeah, I'm sure he had some preconceived notions about me, as I did of him. One day, I somehow lost my star off my outer garment and he asked me if I'd sold it to the Maniac Latin Disciples gang. Losing your star is an offense that could be punishable by termination. So, of course I was freaking out and not in the mood for jokes. He was joking. I mean, I think he was joking. But it didn't take long before I won Bill over and he told me, "You're not so bad, kid."

While I was working with my field training officer, I met this vibrant redhead who looked like a tougher, stronger version of Lindsay Lohan. Her name was Heather Johnson. She had this badass energy about her, yet she still wore lip gloss and mascara like it was nothing. The second I saw her, I thought, *I like this girl. We should be partners.*

I basically stalked her until she finally noticed me, and eventually we started working together. Heather was a former Conner's Angel too, so we instantly clicked. That partnership would last for years. We ended up leaving the 14th District together and joining the Targeted Response Unit, a brand-new, armed-violence suppression, hundred-member team. We made it in, and we kicked ass all over the city of Chicago for the next few years. It was exciting, it was fun, and we got to work alongside some of the best police officers in the department. Heather and I got into some truly crazy situations over the years, and the fact that we're both still here to talk about them sometimes feels like dumb luck mixed with good instincts. This was one of those nights.

We were assigned to the 4th District, which is located on the far South Side of the city. This usually meant long stretches of driving around with nothing happening—just us, the radio, and the low hum of the city after dark. You cruise the same blocks over and over, you watch, you wait. And eventually, if you stay out there long enough, crime finds you. We successfully mapped out every gas station on the South Side that carried a variety of sugar-free beverages. We also took our breaks at whatever twenty-four-hour Walgreens was around to look at magazines and purchase lip gloss. "Balance" was what we always said.

One evening took us onto a stretch of the southbound I-94 highway near 111th Street. At first glance, there's nothing unique about it. Just concrete, traffic noise, sporadic construction, and the CTA bus terminal running alongside the highway. Pretty unremarkable. Cars move through on muscle memory alone, drivers assuming this part of the road is as predictable as the last mile they drove.

But highways lie. They look orderly and controlled until they aren't… until someone panics, someone runs, or someone decides a routine traffic stop is the moment everything changes. And on that stretch of I-94, in the 4th District at 111th Street, that's exactly what happened.

People assume fear is what keeps you sharp in dangerous situations. I've never found that to be true. I don't walk into chaos feeling fearless because I think I'm tougher than anyone else. I walk in steady because I know backup is seconds away. And there is no force on earth more motivated than a police officer racing to help another one. As long as I had my radio and my partner, I trusted that I was going to be okay.

That trust got tested one afternoon when my partner Heather and I conducted a regular traffic stop that went sideways fast. Heather was driving. As soon as we activated our lights and siren, the driver ignored us for a few seconds and got onto the entry ramp to the highway. Moments later, he pulled over to the side of the highway. We radioed the stop in to the dispatcher with the plate information and our location. His vehicle was halfway on the shoulder of the road took when the driver's side door flung open, and out he ran. He took off on foot the second he had the chance. He was at least a foot taller than me, built like he could fold me in half without breaking a sweat. He vaulted over the side of the highway and disappeared into a grassy ravine below… waterlogged, uneven, muddy, and slick. No clear footing. Millions of different ways to break an ankle. No clean angles. Just bad options stacked one on top of the other.

I went after him anyway. This meant I used my best vault technique that I hadn't used in ages and started after him to jump over the guard rail. I was immediately glad that I'd purchased cargo pants a size bigger than my usual size because this meant for easy bending and crouching.

Heather grabbed the female passenger from the front seat, cuffed her, and called for backup as I sprinted toward the bad guy. I was gaining ground, but I knew better than to let adrenaline write checks my body couldn't cash. If I squared up with him alone, it wouldn't end well for me. So I paced myself. I was close enough to keep pressure on him, smart enough to stay alive. I later joked that I stopped and started running in place just to make sure I didn't catch up to him before I was ready. Heather was right where she needed to be, radioing as we moved, calling it out step by step. That's how this works when it works well. One of you runs. The other builds the net.

The guy ran straight into the CTA bus terminal, thinking crowds and cover would save him. Instead, the place was void of people and filled with empty buses. We shut the whole place down. One little button started closing the garage doors. Doors closed. Time slowed. We methodically cleared every single bus and every bit of ground under the buses. Eventually, we found him lying in the back of a bus, hiding on the floor, out of breath and out of options. He was immediately placed into custody without further incident. By the time we grabbed him, we had backup from about twenty-five other officers who were also searching for him. He didn't stand a chance. Turns out he had a warrant. I was aware that he'd probably ditched something while he was running, from the way he was holding his side. We went back to look, but it was something we were never going to find in that mess. Yet none of that mattered. We'd caught him. That day, the good guys won.

Those are the moments people don't always understand: the split-second decisions, the calculated risks, the absolute reliance on your partner and your team. Sometimes, we do crazy things like sprint through ravines alongside highways because standing still isn't an option. You trust your training. You trust your people. And you move.

Back then, we were the elite members of the hundred-member team built for violent crime suppression. That unit was where I learned what real camaraderie looked like. Heather and I were two of the few women on the team, which meant we were often called in for female arrests and searches. Traffic stops brought us together again and again, and that's how I eventually met John Korolis. Not in some dramatic introduction, just work. These types of interactions are the kinds that forge trust.

That unit gave me my love for teamwork. For knowing someone had your back without needing to ask. Looking back, it wasn't the danger that defined those moments. It was the certainty. It was sometimes quiet and unspoken. But I knew that I was never alone out there. I always seemed to land exactly where I needed to be, surrounded by the right people at the right time.

One of those moments happened on a night that should have been forgettable. While processing one of our arrestees in the Englewood District, I met a salty homicide detective named Tim Nolan. I mentioned, almost in passing, that I was studying to become a detective, and somehow that turned into hours of conversation.

Tim talked. I listened. He gave me tips, clues, and the kind of insider advice you don't get from study guides or practice tests. He stressed what mattered, what didn't, and how to think like a detective before you ever wore the title. His guidance helped more than he probably realized. The rest, as they say, is history.

After Heather and I ran into the sunset as members of the Targeted Response Unit, Bill Conners continued to train countless probationary police officers after me. Years later, Bill ended up in hospice care after years of drinking Wild

Turkey and smoking menthol cigarettes had finally caught up to him. Without fail, every one of "Conner's Angels," the title thirty-something years of trainees affectionately gave themselves, showed up to visit Bill and bid their final farewell.

# CHAPTER 9

# GO TO THE VIDEOTAPE

I was slowly starting to fade, so my partner and I decided to stop for some coffee on the way back to Yolanda's residence.

Most Chicago cops love Dunkin' Donuts, but I'm a bit of a coffee snob and prefer coffee from quaint little coffee shops with high charged espresso. If not, Starbucks will do. Anyway, a big pet peeve of mine is coffee places that begrudgingly give cops free coffee. I don't want free coffee. I want a latte with whatever fake milk you have available. The annoyed look they give when you order anything other than a coffee when you're on duty makes me want to tell them, "I'm paying for this! I'm not asking for free coffee." I've even gone as far as covering my badge and gun up so I can order my latte in peace and dodge the comments about there not being any crime in the city today. This is Chicago, fool. There's crime everywhere you look.

I was so glad we'd decided not to release the crime scene. I could come back into Yolanda's apartment and take a few looks around. I was thinking about all of the stacks of paperwork and figured I should look through it and see if I could find any clues in there. I was also going to have to get her phone bills and order her cell phone records. I noticed a landline inside the house, which was surprising. Who has a home phone these days anyway, aside from my mom?

While I was sifting through Yolanda's stuff, my partner went to the property management office and attempted to get any surveillance video from inside and outside the building. I'd noticed a few cameras. Hopefully, one of them had caught the killer entering the building. Minimally, we needed to try and verify Curtis's story and see if he'd really walked in hand in hand with Yolanda. That would also allow me to get a pretty good timeline of what transpired that night.

As I was looking through the paperwork, I grabbed a few bank statements and bills with a cell phone bill. *Score!* I thought to myself. Before I could dig too far into the stacks of mail, my phone started blowing up. I got two text messages from my partner saying come down here, followed by an actual phone call. I said okay and decided to stop what I was doing and run downstairs.

As luck would have it, the surveillance cameras were plentiful and of decent quality for the time, and they were working on the night of the murder.

One thing I've learned in Chicago is chances are if you see a surveillance camera, the likelihood that it's working and pointed in the right direction is usually slim to none. That all changes when a police officer is involved and doing something wrong. Then that camera has night vision, motion sensors, and x-ray vision. For some reason, when a cop does something bad, there is always a camera recording everything. And there's always one stupid guy or gal who messes it up for the rest of us. When people make comments to me about hating the police or eating donuts, I want to ask them if they think all teachers have torrid affairs with their minor students like I heard about on the news? No, of course not. That's absurd. I've seen a few cringey Lifetime movies about that kind of stuff, but I hardly accuse every teacher of being a predator. I wish people would do the same for the police. If I didn't love my job and didn't truly care about people, I surely wouldn't willingly subject myself to so much criticism.

So, I got downstairs and lo and behold, my partner had saved the day! We were looking at the person who might have killed Yolanda or maybe even helped Curtis after he killed Yolanda.

And I say he, because it definitely looked like a dude walking. This person strolled into the building after 4:00 a.m. It looked like he was carrying a bunch of laundry as he walked into the building.

*Hmm, maybe he brought cleanup supplies. Maybe those binoculars were used by Curtis as he looked out the window for his cleanup crew after he killed Yolanda?* I thought to myself.

But judging by the blood in the apartment, it didn't look like anything had been cleaned up. My partner and I sat there with Mr. Dee the building manager, who allowed us to take over his office and play and rewind the video over and over and over and over. We finally asked him to copy the video onto an external USB flash drive for us, and he agreed. We decided we needed to go back to the station at some point and really review this video.

I was very excited now. I needed to solve this case. What I was most excited about was the fact that this guy who walked into the building at 1:00 a.m. didn't use keys or a fob card to get it. I was also excited by the fact that this guy wasn't Curtis. He wasn't tall enough and unless Curtis was wearing seven layers of clothing, this guy was way too heavy to be Curtis. It could be someone Curtis knew, though.

After watching the exterior video surveillance, we were sure someone buzzed the killer into the building. So, that meant Yolanda may have not only known her killer, but she might have unknowingly let him into her house or maybe even worse, Curtis let him in to kill Yolanda. Just when I thought I was done, I decided to run back inside and ask Mr. Dee if he happened to know any of Yolanda's family members, since no one seemed to notice she hadn't been around. No one had attempted to call me regarding this case.

I turned back around and caught Mr. Dee right as he was turning off his office lights. I asked him if he could provide me with any of Yolanda's family members' information.

"Why don't you just call her sister and ask her?" he said.

I pretended I didn't know that she had a sister in case he had any additional information to offer.

Mr. Dee proceeded to tell me that Yolanda's sister worked with her and was actually the owner of the salon. Her sister was also listed as Yolanda's emergency contact.

So now, before I could do anything else, I was forced to break the bad news to John and tell him that even though we were tired, we had to go and try to find some more family. Then we could work on breaking down that video. But first things first.

# CHAPTER 10

## THE LIE BOX

My days off flew by as usual and before I knew it, I was back at the police station trying to get my head wrapped around Curtis's statement and subsequent failed lie detector test.

Anyway, I decided to have a sit down with Greg to go over the results of the test. Thank God he'd decided to accompany Marco, since he knew Marco wasn't a big fan of lie detector tests.

After I logged on and checked my upcoming court notifications for the upcoming weeks and my email, Greg came up to me and said, "You want the bad news or the bad news?" He went on to tell me that after Curtis failed the lie detector test, he was dropped off at home by Greg. Greg was none too happy with him. Greg is a great detective with a stellar reputation for getting the bad guys, but he definitely doesn't have anywhere near the level of patience I have. Greg told me he got into a bit of an argument with Curtis, who insisted on knowing what would happen next. Greg said he kept asking and asking, and Greg finally told him to stop talking.

I asked Greg if we had to worry about Curtis heading back to Jamaica or Jamaica Queens or wherever this guy was really from, and Greg said he didn't have a true read on him. He then proceeded to tell me that Curtis acted like he was shocked when he learned he'd failed the test.

"He insisted on talking to you," Greg said. "I guess he thinks he can try to explain and try to get one over on you."

*No chance, buddy*, I thought to myself. Fool me once, shame on me. You know the rest.

Greg said Curtis then asked him if he would know when they caught the killer. He told Curtis, "You'll know, buddy." And what Greg meant to say was, "You'll know because you'll be wearing shiny bracelets."

Mostly, I was interested in exactly what questions he'd shown deceit in. "What questions did he fail?" I asked.

"What question did he fail?" Greg repeated my question, then followed it by, "What questions didn't he fail?"

Greg then went on to explain that Curtis didn't take a liking to him. I pretended to be shocked, but I wasn't surprised because people either loved or hated Greg, and it was usually the latter for suspects.

Greg said they got into a few heated conversations, and Curtis began referring to Greg as "Mark Fuhrman." For some reason, that really struck a funny bone in me and I couldn't stop laughing. I had to give Curtis credit. That was quite the analogy. Mark Fuhrman was the L.A. cop who investigated the Nicole Simpson and Ron Goldman murders in 1994 and basically was accused of being a lying racist cop with a beef with O.J. Simpson. With murders, I refer to my cases by the victim's name, not the perpetrator. I feel like the bad guys get all the attention as it is. We should never forget the victim. I was pleased with the fact that we had a new nickname for Greg.

Greg said he started by asking Curtis if he'd ever been arrested and he said yes, he had, but when he was asked about specifics he said he didn't do anything and lazy cops "put that case on him." Well, it turned out that Curtis had been arrested for a domestic incident in the past and guess who the victim was? Yep, Yolanda. It looked like

Yolanda had a party at her house for a Floyd Mayweather boxing match, and Curtis showed up uninvited and got into a pissing match with one of her male guests because he was jealous and thought the guy was standing too close to Yolanda. It ended with Curtis getting dragged out of the apartment by the police and taken to jail. And one of the listed witnesses was Yolanda's sister. Weird how no one mentioned this to us before. And per the arrest report, this was all recorded on police body cam, but he claimed it never happened. I immediately looked up reports and saw that he'd been arrested and the case was later thrown out because Yolanda refused to show up at court and wanted the charges dismissed.

This is a common occurrence with victims of domestic violence. At the time, the victims want the offender arrested, but later they decide to get back together and pretend it never happened. And unfortunately, a lot of women end up dead, just like Yolanda. Just because the case was thrown out certainly didn't mean Curtis didn't do it. Curtis was looking more and more like he was responsible for Yolanda's death. I just had to figure out who the hell entered Yolanda's apartment on video. Maybe it was someone Curtis had called. I definitely had to get Curtis's phone records.

# CHAPTER 11

## DETECTIVE LADY

I was back on the case and finally checked my department voicemail. There were six messages—every single one from Curtis, every single one marked URGENT. So of course, I called him back immediately.

Curtis answered on the first ring and practically yelled into the phone that he thought the person who killed Yolanda was coming after him. He was frantic, accusing me of not doing enough to protect him. And I told him probably a little more sharply than I intended that he wasn't doing enough to help me. Let's not forget there was only one eyewitness we knew of: him.

"Help me help you," I told him. In my head, I was thinking, *This dude is going to be a hard nut to crack.*

Curtis said he was just a couple blocks away from the station and needed to talk to us. I told him to come in right away. He showed up within fifteen minutes looking like a complete mess. I placed him in one of the interview rooms, which, of course, doubles as an interrogation room. He immediately started in on me again, insisting I wasn't doing enough to catch the killer.

"Isn't there a video?" he asked. This guy had some serious nerve. Then he casually dropped that Yolanda had briefly dated some shady guy he forgot to mention. Perfect.

Another person to track down, alibi, eliminate. Every time I asked Curtis for help, he handed me more work.

Before I sat down with him, I told him I had to search him. When I asked the standard questions—any weapons, anything illegal, anything that's going to poke or stick me— he laughed. My eyes rolled so hard they almost fell out of my head. If I had a dollar…

I escorted him into the interview room. These rooms aren't meant for comfort. Not for suspects, not for us. I didn't make him sit on the steel bench attached to the wall. I actually found an office chair to wheel into the room. I picked the one with the least brown stains, which is really saying something. I grabbed him a bottle of water from our station "store," which is basically a late-night sugar trap run on the honor system.

There are chips, soda, candy, and those questionable breakfast sandwiches no one touches unless they've been awake for thirty-six hours straight. But sometimes people— witnesses, offenders, and other detectives—need that extra burst of energy. You grab what you need, something to get you through the shift or to hold over your arrestees or witnesses, and drop whatever you think is fair into the jar. Sometimes it's a dollar, sometimes five, depending on what you grabbed. You can't be sure if anyone was watching, but the understanding is simple: you take what you need and pay for it, or you don't, and hope that no one noticed.

It's a small but significant trust exercise, an unspoken agreement that if you don't pay, you'll probably get caught eventually, or worse, you'll ruin it for everyone else. In a place like the Detective Division, where everyone has seen and heard enough to make them a little cynical, it's kind of surprising to see something so basic, so… pure. No one ever wants to be the person who ruins it for everyone.

That jar was a little microcosm of the department's culture—respect and trust, as much as possible—in a place where there wasn't always much of either. I threw a couple dollars in the money jar for the water because I was sure I had a running tab. And I'm a big believer in karma. I'm convinced that if I accidentally steal anything, even a granola bar, I'll pay for it. Fall asleep at the wheel, trip down the stairs, drown in the bathtub, because God punished me for petty theft. No thank you.

Back in the room, I looked at Curtis and said, "Go home and come back when you want to tell me the truth." At this point, I was thinking I would just ask Yolanda's sister about the ex-boyfriend.

Still, I explained to Curtis how badly I needed him to help me if we were going to solve this. He finally agreed to basically join the team, as he put it. Then he immediately asked if he was a suspect. I gave it a few beats before telling him no, he wasn't. Not officially. But was his story believable? Also no. Who's going to believe that a woman was shot and stabbed to death while allegedly sleeping in his arms and he somehow didn't see or hear a thing? He wasn't badly injured. Why would the killer let him walk away? He kept insisting he had no idea what happened.

My teammates were going to love this story. And Curtis, well, he had an original sense of humor, I had to give him that.

Curtis decided to stay a little longer, and I asked him what happened to his hand, which was bruised and swollen. He gave me, in the thickest Jamaican accent I've ever heard, "You, Detective Lady. *You* tell me." Great. Not starting well.

"Hey, you called me," I reminded him.

He apologized and claimed he'd hurt his hand fighting for his woman's life.

"Okay, then tell me everything," I said. And now I was apparently "Detective Lady." I'd been called worse, so fine.

Curtis launched into the entire story of that night. And when I say entire, I mean every microscopic detail, including things I didn't need to hear. He explained that he and Yolanda had a chaotic on-again, off-again relationship, great when it was good, physical when it was bad. But that night, she called him out of the blue asking if he wanted to meet up. He jumped at the chance. He claimed he was a warm-blooded man who couldn't say no to a beautiful woman.

They skipped dinner and went straight for cocktails at a lounge near her place. He got a ride to her apartment to meet up, and they had a phenomenal night. I still couldn't tell if he was a hopeless romantic or completely full of shit. I asked what they drank, but he couldn't remember.

I've learned you can tell a lot about a person by their drink. I used to hate gin. Thought gin drinkers were the type to sit alone in the dark, smoke, and listen to sad music. Then I discovered Negronis by accident. Out of desperation one night I told a bartender, "Make me something good." Ten minutes and half a confession of love later, I asked what was in it.

"Gin," he said.

"GIN?" I yelled. "I don't drink gin."

"Well, now you do," he said.

Leave it to a man to give me exactly what I said I didn't want. And maybe I *am* the type to occasionally sit in the dark and lament about the bad choices I've made in life, just without the cigarettes. Wrinkles and bad breath aren't worth it.

Anyway, Curtis went on and on about how magical the night was. I was sitting there thinking, *Okay, but what really happened?*

"What happened next?" I pressed.

They drove back to Yolanda's place and, in his words, "We made sweet love." If you could have seen my face. Who actually talks like that?

By now, Curtis seemed like the obvious suspect. The story was outrageous. Anyone would assume he'd done it: too many cocktails, he snaps, she won't take him back, and he loses it. Case closed, right? Not so fast. As nauseating as his "sweet love" talk was, something about him made me believe he was telling the truth. He said they fell asleep in each other's arms. Romantic, sure.

"So then what happened?" I asked.

He looked annoyed and said flatly, "I don't know."

My frustration level was rising, but I needed to keep him talking. He finally finished his explanation: while he was asleep, someone came into Yolanda's apartment and shot her in the head. He claimed he had no idea who it was or how it happened.

I stopped him. "So, you're telling me you were in the bed with her when she was shot and killed?"

"Yes."

I asked him nicely if he would sign a consent to dump his cell phone. He hesitated, then agreed. I glanced at my partner, who looked completely bored. I asked if he had questions.

"Nope. You can fill me in later."

Wait, what? John sat through this entire interview and wanted the recap later? Apparently, this interview was boring. I guess he spent the time daydreaming about the accolades he would get when we closed the case. Probably imagined himself walking slow-motion with Curtis in cuffs to the theme song of *Cops*. Not happening. Because he clearly wasn't listening to a thing. That's the problem with being thorough, I guess.

I took Curtis back into the room and had him tell the whole story again. This time, when he got to the part where he "doesn't know" how she got shot, I stopped him and told him straight up: no one—including me—was going to buy that. He insisted he had nothing to do with it.

I was getting irritated. "Curtis," I said, "what happened to Yolanda? You were there. Only you can help me."

And again, in that heavy accent, "YOU, Detective Lady. You tell me."

I stormed out and slammed the door. The walls aren't exactly soundproof, so everyone outside heard. One of the old-timers called out, "Hey, Rookie, when are you gonna cuff the killer?" He pointed to the room where Curtis was sitting.

"Nope," I replied. "He didn't do it." I wasn't saying he was telling the whole truth, but he didn't kill her. I didn't know why I was giving him this much credit, but I was. We decided to end the interview with Curtis and told him we would check back in with him soon. Before Curtis walked out, he smiled, waved, and said, "Talk to her sister."

Then he explained that Yolanda's sister Tiffany worked with her at the hair salon—and the business was actually in her sister's name.

Curtis was argumentative and combative, but he wasn't a killer… or so I thought. And he was lucky I was the one dealing with him, because anyone else would have thrown cuffs on him hours ago.

# CHAPTER 12

## BEAUTY AND THE GREEK

The old-timers at the station coined the nickname for John and me: "Beauty and the Greek." "Oldies" is what we called the seasoned detectives. These were the guys who were just a breath away from retirement, the ones who had been through everything and seen it all. They had the kind of wisdom that came from decades on the job, offering you advice on everything from how to handle a crime scene to how to survive the political side of law enforcement. They were usually willing to pass down the lessons they'd learned over the years—just don't bother asking them for any help that might involve actually doing work that could drag them back into the courtroom after they'd hung up their badge.

Being a detective is a job that keeps on giving. You think you've earned your time off when you finally retire, but the reality is, your cases don't always let you go. It's a strange kind of loyalty, the way these cases never really leave you. You can count on it, in fact: one of your cases will eventually resurface in a retrial. Maybe the Supreme Court throws it out, or there's some new evidence that has been uncovered years later. Either way, you're pulled back into the system. And that means you'll have to come out of retirement to testify. And here's the kicker: you're not getting paid for it. You do it for the "good of justice," they say. But the truth?

It's a lot of free labor that no one warns you about when you sign up for this job.

That's why so many retired detectives go off the grid when they leave the force. They move to some remote place in Montana or Wyoming, far away from everything, just so no one can find them when it's time to serve that subpoena to testify at court on a case they barely remember. It's the only way to avoid the inevitable, to try to live out their golden years without the constant reminder that their work never really ends.

As I was sifting through the file, I decided to look up the morgue report and the subsequent reports from the medical examiner's office. The morgue report simply stated that Yolanda died from multiple injuries, including a gunshot wound to the head and being stabbed multiple times. Because we'd asked for the "deluxe," that meant that they'd swabbed her body for DNA and done a rape kit and finger nail scrapings. Obviously, we would have to get Curtis's DNA to include and exclude him in the evidence. This would be helpful in the event that Curtis was lying.

We were still waiting for phone records. I'd ordered phone records for Yolanda's land line and her personal cell phone in addition to other lines on her account that were used by her son and the hair salon. Cell phone records were a beast to go through in 2012. Technology has come a long way since then. Now, we can figure out where people are when calls are being made. Back in 2012, we could figure out a general location, but it wasn't as precise. And reading the cell phone records was equally as problematic. Cell site locations came by way of latitude and longitude, which meant for every location you would have to Google Map the coordinates to get an idea of where the phone user was located when they were making the call. This made it take forever to complete a cell phone study on one line, much less four or five.

And Yolanda's homicide wasn't the only homicide we'd caught that day. John and I also got what's called a "handout." That's when a case starts as something else other than a homicide, maybe an injury, maybe something suspicious, and another detective handles it, not realizing it's about to become a murder investigation.

We weren't even informed that this case was ours until a few days after the victim died.

This homicide involved a four-month-old baby boy who was a twin. The surviving twin was placed into protective custody because the parents were suspected to have been involved in the baby's death. The medical examiner ruled the four-month-old's death a homicide after discovering multiple injuries in different stages of healing on his body. We were assigned to the case after it was officially ruled a homicide. Baby murders are the worst. Some of the hardest cases you'll ever work are sexual assaults and infant homicides. With sexual assaults, you see the victim's anguish, their pain, their strength, and you know they have to relive it every time they tell their story. With babies… There's just nothing to say. The innocence of it crushes you.

Thankfully, in this case, I didn't have to physically examine the baby's body. Obviously, I had to review the photos and reports, which was slightly less traumatizing. I've only had to physically examine a child a few times in my career, and each one left a hole in my heart I'll never be able to fill.

One of the first times was a little girl named Heaven Sutton, who was the unintended victim of a gang-involved shooting back in 2012. Heaven Sutton was seven years old. That fact alone changed the air in the room. I'd seen bodies before, but this was different. This was the first one that stayed with me. Examining her didn't feel like police work; it felt like trespassing on something sacred. Her smallness was impossible to ignore. Everything about her reminded me of what she should have been doing instead—sleeping, playing, growing up. I remember how careful I was with her, how every movement felt heavier than it should, like my hands were carrying more than just procedure. I told myself to stay professional, to focus, and to do the job the way I was trained. That scene followed me home, into my sleep, into my silence. Heaven was my first, and she quietly taught me something no training ever could: this job would take pieces of me I didn't yet know how to give.

So with Yolanda and the baby… that made two murders with possible domestic angles assigned to John and me in one day.

As we waited for the medical examiner to fax over the "protocol" on the baby, which details the victim's injuries and internal and external exams that were conducted, my mind drifted back to Yolanda and Curtis. This is what I call multi-tasking.

Yolanda's case followed me like a shadow. Something still felt off. I couldn't explain it, but deep down something whispered, *You're missing something.* I knew Yolanda had a history of domestic incidents, but I still couldn't figure out if or how those incidents were related.

People often ask me, "What's the most dangerous type of call police respond to?"

They expect me to say something dramatic like hostage situations, armed robberies, and gang shootouts. They're usually surprised when I tell them the truth. Other than chasing someone with a gun, domestic disturbances are by far the deadliest. The unpredictability, the emotions, the alcohol, the history… everything is already lit before we even arrive. All it takes is a spark.

One of the first calls I ever handled was a domestic. I remember stepping into that apartment and immediately feeling the tension hit me like a wall. The victim was a middle-aged Hispanic woman who was short, tough, and loud. She was clearly somebody who'd spent her life surviving things harder than me showing up at her door.

She'd been beaten by her boyfriend, and it didn't take long to realize they'd both been drinking heavily. She was shaken and bruised, but still alert, talking fast and pacing like she couldn't decide whether to cry or start swinging.

Her boyfriend, on the other hand, was past the point of listening to anyone. By the time we walked in, he was already squared up, hands raised, teeth clenched, ready to fight whoever crossed the threshold. And he didn't hesitate. He lunged straight at the officer next to me, and the two of them went crashing through a glass table like we'd just walked onto the set of a bad action movie. That officer was Frano, a guy who'd won a police boxing competition called Super Cop multiple times. In other words, I wasn't too worried about him.

My assignment was the victim. Not that Frano needed backup anyway; that man could fight in his sleep. My job was to get the basics, like what happened, who hit who, whether she wanted to sign complaints so we could arrest him. The usual process. And I already had that cynical little voice in my head whispering what experience eventually proved true: she would probably be back with him before the first court date. But still… part of you always hopes maybe today will be the day someone chooses differently.

And here's the twist most people never believe until they see it: the victim suddenly jumped in, not to help us, but to defend him. One second, she was standing next to me, giving me the rundown; the next moment, she was flying across the room trying to pull Frano off her boyfriend. I was completely caught off guard. I grabbed her to keep her from getting hurt or making things worse, but it was like a mosquito hitting a bug zapper. She bounced right off him. He didn't even notice.

That wasn't the last 911 call from that residence. Not by a long shot. And it was my first real lesson in how complicated, volatile, and downright heartbreaking domestic disturbances can be. You think you're walking into a simple rescue, but half the time you realize the danger is coming from every direction, which includes from the people you're trying to help.

# CHAPTER 13

# NEVER TAKE THE SAME ROUTE HOME

I was home in my bed, comfy and trying to fall asleep to an episode of *Law & Order*, but for some reason I kept waking up. So, I tried to go back to sleep but was abruptly woken up several times by the same bad dream I had almost every night. I could always describe the dream right when I woke up but poof, then it was gone and the memory was dim. It was something about forgetting to take my medicine, even though I never took any medicine other than a random Z-Pack here and there. Calling it a nightmare is to say the least. This was a full blown night terror. All I know is that I was scared. I tried to keep a journal next to my bed or talk myself out of the terror, but it never worked. But some of my toughest cases were solved from my bed at 3:00 a.m. post nightmare.

As I walked into work, I was very aware of how loud my heels sounded today. Maybe I had a little extra pep in my step. The office wasn't as loud as it usually was. There was chatter here and there, but no one was in custody and no one was playing the typical loud police pursuit videos from YouTube.

A few detectives in the office didn't purposely turn around to look at me as I walked in and proceed to yell, "Michele's here," in a playful manner. Am I the only one with a distinctive walk? I've had this walk since I was a kid. In fact, when I was a teenager, a crude guy whom I declined an offer of a date with used to quack like a duck when I walked by. I guess he thought I'd never heard that before. I still have a little bit of the duck walk, but it's a more refined now.

I like to wear wedges or boots that kind of click when I walk, and I'm told I walk like a horse. I'm not sure what it is with the comparison of animals. But I like horses, so it could be worse.

Greg was sitting at his desk feverishly typing with just two fingers. He stopped to look over at me and said, "You make a lot of noise for such a little girl." He proceeded to get up and imitate what he refers to as the "Michele walk." He got up, pushed his butt out, and shook it while he stomped. I've got to admit, he did a stellar job at it.

Okay, I admit it. I walk very hard. It's like everything I do. Nothing soft going on here.

I sat at my desk and did my daily ritual of cleaning the phone and keyboard with bleach wipes. I wiped some sticky brown gunk from the desk and emptied out the crumbs stuck inside the keyboard. Then I took a stroll around the office and attempted to locate my special chair, which someone had moved from my desk. I found another one that would do for the time being and rolled it over to my desk.

I decided that I would have to wait for some of the evidence to come back before I could even think about figuring out exactly what had happened to Yolanda. I figured I would dive headfirst into the evidence and crime scene photos today... but then just like that, my sergeant came up and said, "Sorry, guys. I know you have a lot of work to do, but a murder just came in and it's yours." He seemed almost excited to tell us this bad news. I thought I even detected a smile.

At that time, I was neck-deep in the Yolanda Holmes homicide. This included sleepless nights, fresh crime scenes, and interviews that ran into the morning. And in the middle of all that chaos, I got pulled into court for the Green Dolphin Murder of Carlos Aguirre.

The case itself doesn't stand out in my memory, at least not compared to some of the others I've had. Same courtroom air thick with disinfectant and nerves, same bench of witnesses avoiding my eyes, same prosecutor flipping through exhibits like we'd been doing this forever.

But what does stand out... is a conversation. A single sentence that has stayed with me ever since.

That day, I was tasked with keeping an eye on one of the witnesses before the trial started. This meant basically babysitting him to make sure he didn't bolt. Although even if he did show up, the risk of him not showing up, changing his story, or disappearing altogether was real.

This was a gangland murder... the murder of Carlos Aguirre. It happened outside the Green Dolphin nightclub, one of those places that used to pulse with Chicago nightlife, a mix of glitter, danger, and everything in between. Back in the day, it had been a legit jazz club—dim lights, velvet booths, saxophones spilling out onto the street, the whole classic scene. But as jazz started dying out and the crowds got younger, the place reinvented itself. Out went the smooth trumpet solos, in came the DJs, bottle service, and enough strobe lights to trigger a seizure. It had that confused identity thing going on: part classy nostalgia, part "who let all these twenty-somethings in here?"

By the time I got the call for the murder, the club vibe had fully taken over. The neon sign still said Green Dolphin, but the soul of the place had shifted. The jazz stage where legends once played was now the backdrop for a DJ booth drowning in bass. The old mahogany bar was sticky with spilled vodka Red Bulls. The air smelled like a mix of cheap perfume, Fabuloso floor cleaner, cigarettes, and whatever was left of the building's history fighting for its life. What used to be a place with live jazz had been swallowed up by

VIP ropes and sad, half-deflated balloons. Jazz had packed up and left. Chaos had taken over the lease.

Crime scenes in nightclubs are their own special hell. They mean dark corners, too many hands touching too many things, and a layer of grime that no amount of bleach can remove. This one was no exception. The music was still pulsing faintly when I walked in, the kind of low thump that rattles in your chest even after the sound system has been turned off. The overhead lights flickered as we found our way to the back office, where the manager was waiting for us.

People were hysterical, clumped together in little groups. Half of them were drunk, while the other half pretended they weren't drunk. Security was pacing like they already knew they were getting blamed for everything.

The victim was slumped dead in his SUV, just down the street from the entrance. His female companion was inconsolable.

We tracked down plenty of witnesses, but most of them were part of the lifestyle, which meant court was a hard no. Statements were one thing. Showing up under oath was another. Eventually, we got one guy to come in. He'd been there that night, and he was the only person who could tell the whole story because he was friends with both the victim and the guy who pulled the trigger.

It turned out the murder of Carlos Aguirre wasn't the result of a random act of violence or a deal gone bad, but something far more personal. Jose Melecio didn't just know Carlos… they moved in the same circles, shared the same spaces, and trusted many of the same people. They'd even gone to the nightclub together that night. That familiarity is what made the night unravel so quickly. What started as a joke about who was paying the bill turned into confrontation, and then into a decision that couldn't be taken back. By the time Carlos was left dead, the damage was already done not just to one life, but to everyone connected to both men. The case was less about who pulled the trigger and more about how inevitability creeps in when loyalty, ego, and violence all collide in the same room.

So, after we got the witness to show up to the trial, I sat with him. I talked. I tried to make it feel normal, even though nothing about it was. He was a rapper. Of course he was. It felt like every gang member I met during that stretch had a mixtape and a dream. But this one was different. He actually had talent. A real following. People knew his name. I could see it clearly: in another version of his life, one small turn to the left, he might have ended up somewhere else entirely.

He was confident, street-smart, a little too slick for his own good. We talked about old Chicago House Music, our favorite hip hop artists, dumb things to pass the time. I've always been good at reading people, and with him, it was easy to see both sides: the hustler and the dreamer.

Then the conversation shifted. He started asking me little personal questions, casual at first. Nothing out of line, but enough to make me notice. Where do you live? How far is your drive home? Do you go the same way every night? I remember kind of laughing, brushing it off. And that's when he looked me dead in the eye and said, "Didn't anyone ever tell you? Never take the same route home." It stopped me cold. It wasn't a threat. It wasn't even advice, really. It was more like he was stating a fact. Street wisdom. Like I should already know this.

Now, I'd heard versions of that before. Every cop has. But the way he said it—calm, matter-of-fact—it landed differently. It wasn't paranoia to him. It was a survival instinct, something that kept him alive long enough to be sitting in that courthouse with me. And I realized, in that moment, I was a creature of habit. I liked routine. Same gas station. Same exit. Same left turn off the Kennedy. I told myself it was fine because I stayed alert, always scanning mirrors, always watching for tails. But still… after that day, I couldn't shake his voice or his advice.

Every night when I left work, I thought about that line. Sometimes, I would turn a different way, just to see how it felt. Other times, I would take the long route, make an extra turn down an empty block, just to test the theory. It wasn't fear. It was something subtler… curiosity. Awareness. A reminder that someone out there might be watching, even when you think no one is.

That witness probably never thought twice about that conversation again. For him, it was small talk in a holding room before testifying. And he did, in fact, testify. A verdict of guilty of first-degree murder was secured largely because of him. But for me, it stuck. It carved out a little corner in my brain, the kind of thing that echoes back at random times. When you catch your reflection in a dark window. When a car's been behind you just a little too long.

It's funny how the lessons that stay with you the longest don't come from the police academy or police manuals or even your mentors. They come from the people you least expect, the people you're trained not to trust. And sometimes, those are the lessons that save you.

I like to think of myself as pretty low-maintenance, but I do have limits. Feet are one of them. I've seen too many of them in too many conditions to ever find them relaxing, endearing, or deserving of lotion. This isn't a preference; it's trauma. And I'm not even talking about the worst ones. Just know this: if foot rubs are your love language, I am not your girl. I respect hard work, loyalty, and effort, but your toes are going to have to fend for themselves. When we make an arrest, one of the first things we do is tell the suspect to take off their shoes. You would be surprised at what people hide in there. Shoes are a perfect place to stash things: drugs, knives, lighters, whatever they don't want anyone to find. So, we literally have to take the shoe off, check the insole, shake it out, and make sure there's nothing hidden. It's a quick routine, but it's necessary, because a little bit of ingenuity goes a long way when it comes to hiding contraband. All it takes is one clever spot, one spot no one thinks to look, and that's where they'll stash their illegal goods.

But let me tell you something: there are some smells in this job that would shock you. I've smelled some things that would make a person gag. Feet. Oh, the feet I've encountered. There's a certain stench that lingers in your nose long after you've left the scene, a smell worse than a rotting dead body. And I don't mean to be graphic, but some of the worst offenders are the guys who spend $200 on a pair of sneakers—gym shoes, as we call them in Chicago—and still don't think to wash their filthy feet. How someone can drop that kind of cash on a pair of shoes and not take the time to scrub off the grime from their own feet? I'll never understand it. You would think if you're going to spend money on something that's going to be wrapped around your feet all day, the least you could do is keep the damn things clean. So, no, I'm not rubbing anyone's feet. I've seen enough to last a lifetime… and then some.

Prisoners can be very creative with hiding stuff, and not just in shoes. I once had a guy in custody who was locked in an interview room and kept popping up with cigarettes. And I mean new, lit cigarettes, not a piece of a cigarette butt he found discarded on the floor.

I kept smelling smoke over the course of several hours and would open the door and there he was smoking a cigarette. I assumed another detective felt sorry for the guy and was giving him smokes. But I finally figured out this guy had stuck a whole pack of Newports up his butt... lighter and all, before the cops got the cuffs on him. Booty dope is expected, but booty cigarettes? Who wants to smoke that?

The cigarette-loving guy was going to the county jail for failing to register as a child sex offender, and he knew he was headed for trouble. No one likes sex offenders, especially in jail. Even worse for him was the fact that he was a convicted child sex offender. He thought if he had some cigarettes, he could use it as a bargaining tool to NOT get his ass kicked every day, a bribe, if you will. I finally got the whole box from him and literally had to wash my hands with bleach to get rid of the nastiness.

# CHAPTER 14

# GOLDEN RULES

I live by what I call the Golden Rules of being a homicide detective. Not because I'm some enlightened guru on a mountaintop but because without rules, this job will chew you up and spit out whatever's left. People think homicide is all blood and evidence bags and dramatic one-liners. Sure, but only sometimes. Mostly? It's grief. And chaos. And trying to stay human while chilling with the worst parts of humanity.

So, the Golden Rules keep me sane… or at least functioning.

**1. Have thick skin.**

People will hate you for showing up. They'll hate you for asking questions. They'll hate you because someone they love is dead and you're the person standing there with a notebook instead of a miracle.

**2. Treat people like humans, no matter how barbaric they act.**

This is harder than it sounds. The screaming, the threats, the lies. I've learned it's all just pain wearing different masks.

**3. Do yoga.**

Seriously. Pretend you're stretching for health, but really, you're preventing yourself from choking out your coworkers.

**4. Don't tell people to fuck off—especially on video.**

This one is self-explanatory. Body cameras are the real villains in some stories.

**5. No one will ever be happy to see you.**

Homicide detectives only meet you when:

- You're dead;

- Someone you love is dead;

- You watched someone else become dead; or

- You're the reason someone is dead.

Not exactly the welcome wagon.

**6. Find humor with your friends.**

Laugh every day so you don't cry yourself to sleep every night. Dark humor is the only currency we accept in this profession.

These rules don't make me perfect, but they make me better.

Let's get into my specialty: **confessions.**

My lieutenant and mentor told me way back when that I have a unique, unorthodox way of getting people to talk. One older detective once said, "Wood, you could get a confession out of a brick wall." I took it as a compliment.

Is there a bat of the eye? A smile?

Sure. I'm not dead inside… yet.

But it's more than that.

It's everything I learned from the twenty or so random jobs I had before joining the department—bartending, waitressing, being a flight attendant and an aerobics instructor. Every job was anthropology. Human Behavior 101. And all of it carved out my method.

First Rule of the Method: **The Interview Shirt.**

The interview shirt is tight enough to show you have a pulse, but not tight enough to be accused of using your pulse as an interrogation tactic. There's a razor-thin line between confident and skanky. Stay on the right side of it.

Flirtation? Maybe. But it's not sexual, it's strategic. It's friendliness. Warmth. A flicker of comfort in a cold room. You give a smile, you offer safety, and they forget you're the one who cuffed them.

Second Rule of the Method: **Never Lose Control of the Interview.**

- Never let the offender think they have the upper hand.

- But also… don't disrespect them.

- Let them talk. Let them explain. Let them paint themselves into the corner. Because liars always talk too long.

- They get nervous, they ramble, and somewhere in that babble, the truth slips out like a drunk confession at 2:00 a.m.

And when you listen closely and pay attention, you'll hear it.

What really seals the deal, though, is a little bit of psychological Stockholm syndrome. Think about it: the detective is the captor. I take their freedom. I close the door. I control the room.

My job is to make them want *me*.

Not like that—get your mind out of the gutter. I mean want *my presence*.

By the end of the interview, they're knocking on the door asking for me because they want to "explain." They want to "set the record straight." They want to tell *me* their side because everyone else in their life has stopped listening. It works. Not once or twice. A LOT. More often than anyone wants to admit.

People are people. Men are men. Women are women. Everyone wants to be heard. Everyone wants to control the narrative—even when the narrative is self-incriminating.

Speaking of being heard…

Everyone… including homicide detectives… wants to be heard in their personal life...

So, what about dating as a female homicide detective? Simple: **you don't.**

In my experience, there are three types of men:

**1. Men who want to sleep with a cop.**

They think it's hot. They have fantasies involving handcuffs that absolutely don't comply with department policy.

**2. Men who swear they would *never* touch a cop.**

This group is the loudest and the most insecure. Big "I'm totally not intimidated by you but actually I am" energy.

**3. The Unicorn.**

The rare man who is so comfortable in his masculinity that he's not threatened by a woman who carries a gun, sees murder scenes, and could technically kill him and maybe even cover it up if she wanted to. (Hypothetically speaking, of course.)

The unicorn doesn't mind if the woman beside him has power. In fact, he kind of likes it. Confidence is its own kind of pheromone.

Over the years, I've learned that people tend to lie in remarkably similar ways. That observation hasn't made me cynical; it has made me careful. I approach certain cases with a healthy amount of skepticism—not because I doubt victims, but because experience has taught me that patterns exist. And it's important to say this plainly: unbelievable things do happen, and real victims deserve to be heard and protected. My instincts aren't about disbelief; they're about discernment.

Long before I became a detective, I was being trained for the job without realizing it. As a waitress and a flight attendant, my days were spent keeping people comfortable, reading the room, and learning who people were through small talk. Interviewing isn't all that different. You listen. You watch. You learn how people from every walk of life communicate under stress. Somewhere along the way, I also learned how people bullshit, how people lie, and how people tell the truth.

Working as a detective, you start to notice patterns. One that shows up again and again is the classic "stranger danger" scenario, often involving a white van… with no windows. For some reason, when people lie, they tend to lie the same way. The details repeat. The script sounds familiar.

There are plenty of reasons people make false police reports. Sometimes, it's a kid caught past curfew who panics and needs a believable excuse. Other times, it's a cheating spouse who gets caught and spins a wild story in a moment of desperation. Usually, we figure it out fairly quickly, but you have to walk a fine line, because every now and then, the most unbelievable story turns out to be true.

That said, I can't tell you how many times I've heard some version of this: an unknown offender in a white van with no windows, a blindfold placed over the victim's eyes, a noxious substance over their mouth causing them to pass out, followed by robbery or assault, and then conveniently being dropped back home. I'm not saying stranger abductions don't happen. They absolutely do. I just don't know why this particular storyline gets reused so often when someone isn't being honest.

Ask any cop with more than a little time on the job, and I bet they'll tell you a similar version of this story.

# CHAPTER 15

# DEADLIFTS AND DEAD BODIES

I started competitive fitness and bodybuilding back in 2005, four years into the Chicago Police Department. At first, it was just a break, a chance to wear high heels, spray tan, and makeup, which, in my line of work, felt like a rebellion. But it quickly became a full-blown obsession, a grind that demanded as much discipline as any criminal investigation. Somehow, I was balancing two worlds that couldn't have been more different: the gym and the streets.

Balancing homicide work with competitive bodybuilding wasn't just time-consuming. It sometimes felt like I was living two completely separate lives that happened to share the same body. One minute, I was stepping over pools of blood and navigating the chaos of someone's final moments, and the next I was slipping into four-inch heels, worried about bikini color choices, macro counts, and whether my spray tan looked too orange under stage lights. It shouldn't have worked. But somehow, it did.

Bodybuilding started as a little rebellion against the grime and intensity of police work, an excuse to be feminine in a world where everything about me had to be tough, armored, and kind of boring. But it quickly turned into something much bigger. The grind, the structure, the way every meal and workout had a purpose... it hooked me. Training gave me something to control when so much of detective work was about managing the uncontrollable.

I would be at a crime scene, breathing through my mouth while examining a decomposing body in one of those old SROs—single room occupancies that were barely big enough for a bed and a chair. These places were usually filthy, the kind of filth that clings to your clothes and follows you home no matter how long you shower. Chicken-wire ceilings, thin makeshift walls, the smell of stale air and old lives. It was never pretty.

One afternoon, I was standing over a man who had clearly been gone for a while. Blood spatter on the wall, flies circling like they owned the place, the whole room frozen in whatever moment ended his life. I was focused, taking it all in, when my phone buzzed in my pocket. Of course, it was Karen Pang, my Canadian partner in crime from the bikini competition circuit. While I was staring at a decomposed body, she was sending me photos of competition bathing suits and asking whether she should go with rhinestones or keep it simple this season. She had perfect timing like that.

I stepped to the side, trying to find the least disgusting square foot of floor, and glanced at the screen. "What are you doing?" she wrote. I typed back "at work" with one hand, my other hand resting instinctively on my gun belt as a fly buzzed past my face. The contrast between our worlds never failed to crack me up. If she only knew what I was looking at while giving her fashion advice.

Karen and I met traveling from show to show and clicked instantly, sharing hotel rooms, tanning products, and last-minute pep talks. Karen would usually do my makeup, which cut down on the expense of competing. Sometimes, we even ended up competing against each other, but it never mattered. We had that weird sisterhood that only comes from too many early mornings, too much protein powder, and too many rhinestones. So there I was, juggling homicide and hemlines, decomposition and designer bikinis… all in a day's work.

Our friendship became one of the strangest but most grounding parts of that chapter of my life. We were two driven, competitive women from different countries who understood the madness of prep life. Hotel rooms, food scales, posing practice in bathroom mirrors, and gossip exchanged between spray-tan sessions. Karen and I shared all of it. And she was a lifeline. She reminded me that there were people in the world who weren't constantly thinking about death.

Competition prep was its own kind of brutality. Every year, like clockwork, I started dieting the first Monday in February, which is usually right after the NFL Super Bowl. No exceptions, no excuses. From that day until September, my life narrowed down to chicken breasts, asparagus, gallons of water, and a mental tunnel vision most people don't understand. I tracked every calorie as religiously as I documented evidence. I meal-prepped with the same intensity I used to interrogate suspects. Every rep, every bite, every hour in the gym mattered.

And yet, despite the exhaustion, I loved it: the stage, the transformation, the control. It kind of felt like stepping into another identity, one where the worst thing that could happen wasn't a homicide victim or a grieving mother; it was someone being leaner or more polished than me. It was a world where goals were clear, rules were straightforward, and outcomes depended on discipline instead of luck or human cruelty.

Fitness didn't just give me something to do outside the job; it saved my sanity. It let me breathe in a way I didn't even realize I needed. It reminded me that I was more than the badge, the cases, and the endless trauma that seeped into the cracks of my life. On days when I couldn't shake a crime scene or the face of a victim, Karen would send a ridiculous meme or a picture of a new bikini she was designing, and suddenly the world didn't feel so heavy.

Over time, I realized that bodybuilding was teaching me skills that made me better at my real job. The discipline. The focus. The ability to push past discomfort and keep going. The confidence to walk into any room, whether it was a stage or a crime scene, and know I belonged there.

In the end, the competitions weren't just about trophies or the stage lights. They were about skills that carried back into my work as a detective. They reminded me that I could compartmentalize, manage chaos, and still find joy and vanity in a world that was often dark, dirty, and brutal. And when the next case came in, I could face it.

Years later, Karen moved to Los Angeles to pursue her dream of becoming a big-time Hollywood makeup artist. She was completely self-taught, one of those naturally gifted people who could transform a face the way some people paint landscapes. Karen started off doing all of the fitness competitors' makeup for fun, but then quickly realized she really had a special talent. But she wasn't one to show up unprepared, so she went out and got every certification Hollywood wanted, stacked them like armor, and walked straight into that world like she belonged there.

My friendship with Karen was always sunlight in my life. No matter how dark things got on the job, no matter how heavy the cases weighed on me, she was this bright, steady reminder that there were good people in the world. People who didn't live inside constant trauma. People who didn't define their days by crime scenes or victim statements. Every few months or so, when I could get some time off, I would fly out to L.A. to visit her, and those trips became my only true escapes. For a few days at a time, I could pretend I was just a normal person, not a detective who carried other people's grief around like extra weight in my pockets.

Karen loved to tell me all about her Hollywood adventures, her celebrity clients, celebrity dates, chaotic photo shoots, and the strange and glamorous behind-the-scenes world she was suddenly part of. And in return, I gave her the PG-13 version of my Chicago cases, the ones that wouldn't haunt her dreams. Karen was a kindhearted Canadian, all soul and empathy. She never truly understood how people could be so cruel or cold. She would shake her head, wide-eyed, horrified at the things I saw every day.

"Dude, you need to quit that job," she always told me. In her world, cruelty didn't make sense; in mine, it was just a regular Tuesday.

L.A. itself felt like a different universe. No one there cared what I did for a living. No one knew I spent my days stepping over bodies or tracking down killers. I wasn't "Detective Wood" in L.A. I was just Michele. Karen and I would hit the gym, go to whatever new restaurant everyone was raving about, and squeeze in an In-N-Out Burger on a random splurge night, laughing like teenagers sneaking out past curfew.

Karen lived with her roommate, Torrie Wilson, the WWE legend. Torrie and I became fast friends too. She was warm, funny, and so unbelievably grounded for someone who had spent years performing in front of millions. Being around the two of them felt like exhaling for the first time in months. They were these gorgeous, vibrant women with big personalities and even bigger hearts. Every trip to L.A. felt like stepping into a softer version of life, a version where my guard didn't have to stay up and my shoulders could actually loosen.

But then, in March 2021, came the phone call that shattered all of it.

I was home in Chicago feeding my newborn daughter when Torrie called me one night. I remember the tone of her voice before the words even landed. I remember her saying, "This is so hard."

I said, "It's okay, Torrie. Just say it." That instinct cops develop… the sound, the silence, the breath before devastation… I felt it instantly. She told me Karen had gone to Colorado on a snowmobiling trip with some of her beautiful fitness friends. A fun getaway, something she'd done before. Karen was from Vancouver, so she was actually a pretty skilled skier and drove snowmobiles all the time. So, it wasn't anything I would have been worried about. And then the words I still can't believe were spoken out loud: Karen hit a tree. The impact killed her instantly.

For a second, everything just… stopped. My stomach dropped. My brain refused to process it. Karen, with her sunshine laugh. Karen, with her endless heart. Karen, who never hurt anyone in her life. Gone.

There are deaths you learn to live with in this job, senseless murders, tragic accidents, the daily reminders that life can disappear in a blink. You develop armor for the world's worst moments because you don't have a choice. But losing Karen? That pierced through every layer. It wasn't a case. It wasn't a stranger. It was one of the only pieces of light I had.

I still can't think about Karen without feeling that pain sharpen in my chest. So I don't. I put it aside. I tuck it away in the mental drawer where the hurts go when they can't be held. It doesn't mean it's gone. It just means it's too heavy to carry all the time.

And that was the moment L.A. stopped being an escape. The city didn't change, but what it held for me did. The joy, the freedom, the sunlight… It all vanished with one phone call.

I went back to L.A. to say goodbye to Karen, and I haven't been back since.

Some losses don't ever heal. You simply learn to keep moving, even with the crack still there.

# CHAPTER 16

# WHEN IT'S WARM, PEOPLE DIE

I was wary of diving too far into my case because today was a warm day, and when it's warm, people die. That's not me being dramatic. There is a very real, very direct correlation, at least in Chicago, between the weather and the crime rate. Anyone who has worked the streets here will tell you the same. The first warm day of the year is historically one of the deadliest, like the whole city has been holding its breath through winter and finally exhales in one violent, chaotic rush. Cabin fever mixed with bad decisions never ends well.

I've seen so many Chicago mayors get on television and say that the weather has nothing to do with murders. My response is always the same: Huh? It absolutely does. In Chicago, our winters are so brutal that sometimes they really do keep people inside. The snow, the cold, the kind of wind that slices right through your coat can quiet a city down. But the first warm day of the year? That's when things shift. That's when everything starts moving again. And unfortunately, that movement often ends in violence.

In a way, it has less to do with the actual weather and more to do with what we call the street temperature. The street temperature isn't about degrees or forecasts. It's a feeling. It's the pulse of the city. You can't read it on a thermometer, but you can feel it in your bones. When you drive around the West Side, or Englewood, or any pocket of Chicago where emotions simmer just beneath the surface, you can sense it. The air itself feels heavier. There's tension you can't quite name: anger, aggression, sadness, loneliness, all of it swirling together, waiting for something or someone to ignite it. And it usually gets ignited when it's warm outside.

So, the temperature is surface-level explanation. We used to joke about "taking a drive to see what the street temperature is," but it wasn't really a joke. It was our ritual, our early warning system. You learned more from one slow roll down a city block than you ever did from a roll call briefing. Mike Galligan, one of the sharpest detectives I've ever worked with, coined the phrase "street temperature," and it stuck.

See, the *weather* can be cold, snow blowing sideways, icicles hanging off street signs, and the *street temperature* can still be burning hot. Or it can be eighty-five degrees, sunshine, and parks full of kids, and the street temperature is flatlined, quiet as a church. They often go hand in hand, but not always. Street temperature is its own animal.

So what is it? It's hard to define because it's not one thing, it's a mix. It's the attitude in the air, the tension on the corners, the way people are moving, talking, yelling, or not yelling. Some days, the temperature is up because of the weather. Those first warm days when everyone who has been cooped up all winter pours outside with their grudges and their booze and their short tempers. But other days, the temperature spikes for reasons no weatherman can explain.

Maybe a big case just went to trial, and one side of the neighborhood is pissed off. Maybe someone high up in the gang hierarchy just got out of prison, and they're trying to reassert control. Maybe a shooting happened the night before, and you can practically feel the retaliation in the air. Or sometimes, it's not anger at all. Sometimes, it's stress, or fear, or politics boiling over, or neighborhoods feeling ignored, or the kind of desperation you can taste but can't quite name. You drive through with your windows cracked just enough and you feel it, like static in your hair or a bad smell that won't go away.

Everyone started using the phrase "street temp" because it was dead-on accurate. The street temperature tells you what's coming before the call ever hits the radio. It's not science, but it's not superstition either. It's instinct. It's experience. It's knowing the city so well you don't have to see trouble to know it's right around the corner. You can feel its heartbeat change. And when that heartbeat starts racing… when the street temperature climbs and everything is uneasy or on edge… you know a murder's about to come in.

And on days like today, with the sun out and the air warm and that familiar hum under the surface, I could feel it already. But tonight, so far, I'd almost escaped without any death. Almost. Which meant I could finally turn my attention back to Yolanda Holmes.

Yolanda and her ex had been involved in altercations more than a few times over the years, which wasn't completely out of the ordinary for a complicated relationship, but enough to put him on my radar. Still, in my eyes, this boyfriend had no real motive to kill her. Something about it didn't fit. I needed someone who knew Yolanda beyond the arguments and the paper trail. I needed to find a real friend, someone she trusted, and someone who could tell me who she was when no one was watching.

Because cases like this didn't crack open from reports; they cracked open from people and from hitting the pavement, like we in Chicago always say. I knew the other guys on my team were fairly confident the killer was Curtis, but something in my head was telling me to make sure I wasn't missing something.

I started getting returns on the phones. So far, Curtis's phone looked clean as a whistle. I still had lots of questions and wanted to talk to him again. John didn't believe Curtis's story one bit, but before I could say I believed him, I had to compare all of that blood evidence from the hall to Curtis and Yolanda and whoever else was there. I assumed that the blood was Yolanda's. But could it be Curtis's blood too?

John was busy doing everything but police work. He was looking up real estate in the area and listening to Lady Gaga. Of course, he was playing it a little too loud and annoying everyone on the floor.

"Let's go pick up Curtis," I suggested.

John agreed, and I proceeded to wait thirty minutes while he "gunned up." John always came to work with his revolver on his ankle but left his duty semi-automatic in his locker. So, I had to wait until he went to the locker room and he was locked and loaded.

"Hurry up, John," I said out loud. "I don't want to be here all night." I'd agreed to pick Curtis up on the corner a few blocks from the station. John moves at his own pace, but he also has the patience of a saint. He's the yin to my yang.

I could see Curtis in the distance, pacing and running his fingers through his hair as he feverishly looked around, paranoia in his eyes. Before we allowed him entry in my car, John searched him to make sure he didn't have any weapons or contraband. I then jumped into the back seat with Curtis and asked John to drive around for a bit.

Curtis finally admitted that he hadn't been completely truthful with us. He told me that when Yolanda was attacked, he'd actually heard someone come into her apartment. He said he "may have" been crouched down on the side of the bed, on the floor, trying to get his bearings when the shot went off. He was half asleep, confused, and trying to figure out what was happening when the killer realized he was there and basically tried to beat him to death.

At first, Curtis said he didn't see the guy's face because the attacker wore a hoodie with the strings pulled tight around his face, and the room was pitch black. The fight spilled into the hallway and, according to Curtis, he was fighting for his life. That's when the hoodie was pulled back during the fight and he got a look straight into the killer's eyes. Curtis told me he was bleeding from his face and head and had no idea what to do because he was losing the fight. Then he said he was ashamed because he knew Yolanda had been killed and he couldn't help her.

I hate to admit it, but I believed the poor bastard. What he was saying actually made sense, and it could explain why he'd failed the lie detector test.

We sent all of the evidence from the scene to the Illinois State Crime Lab for comparison, and so far, the only thing we'd learned was that none of the blood in the hallway belonged to Yolanda. It was all Curtis's, meaning his injuries were a lot bloodier, and probably a lot worse, than they'd appeared when we first met him on scene. So, these revelations were actually corroborating Curtis's statement of events.

I told Curtis that I needed him to try to recall details about the killer. Did he say anything? Did Curtis recognize anything about him? Did Curtis smell anything, feel anything that could help us to identify him?

"Curtis, you have to help me."

Well, Curtis went back to being Curtis and started losing his patience with me. I'd had enough back and forth, so we took him right back to where we'd picked him up from. I told him to think about what we'd talked about and come back tomorrow with some answers. I asked John to drop him off and head back into "the barn," as John loves to call it.

We'd submitted several items for processing, but so far none of them had come back with any foreign DNA. We were still waiting on one interesting item, a single earbud from a pair of headphones recovered in the apartment. Initially, this item had been overlooked. We were hoping that little thing was our smoking gun. We believed the earbud had come off the killer during the death match between Curtis and him. Only time would tell.

The next day when I got to work, since I was on a roll, I decided to make a quick call to Tiffany and ask her about Yolanda's son Qaw'mane. Tiffany seemed oddly annoyed by my call and proceeded to tell me that Qaw'mane was out of control spending money. She hadn't seen him for a while.

I decided to call John ahead of time to let him know to eat something before he got to work. This would avoid him insisting that he was starving to death and going to die. Men are babies when they're hungry. You would think I'm his wife—or worse, his mom—the way he thinks I'm supposed to cater to his needs when he's hungry or thirsty or tired. That's where the term "Work Wife" comes in, I guess. I called John and told him to be at work at 4:00 p.m., so I could expect him to walk in sometime after 5:15.

Lucky for me, Yolanda's phone records came in. I'd literally ordered phone records for her cell phone, her home phone, and basically the phone of anyone she'd contacted on the day of her murder. Now I needed some time, space, and freedom to really study these records and see what they meant.

Now, if only John would sit still for a minute, we could go through these stacks of phone records.

I started the harrowing task alone. I immediately noticed Curtis's cell phone number, as well as Yolanda's son Qaw'mane's numbers. He had two cell phones, one registered to him and one registered to Yolanda. There were a few other numbers that I needed to figure out who they belonged to. Hopefully, the killer's number was in there somewhere. I mean, the killer somehow got her code to enter her apartment building, so I knew he probably knew Yolanda, but how?

The second I walked in, my sergeant said, "Don't get too comfortable. You're up!"

I literally had zero time to actually work on this murder. "YOU'RE UP!" is the worst thing you can hear when you're trying to get into the zone to work on a case. It meant that the next murder that came in was mine. Hopefully, it would be cold and everyone would stay inside today. Strike that. Yolanda had stayed inside, and she was murdered. So, I just hoped no one killed anyone and left it at that.

Sitting there going through these photo records was exhausting yet boring. I immediately saw a few phone numbers that I could guess were those of her closest friends and family members because they kept popping up over and over. Man, did she love to send text messages. There were literally 10,000 text messages sent this month. I hear the average is 3000 to 4000, so she was doing more than double that. I had a shit load of Yolanda's bills and mail in front of me. I sifted through it and discovered that Yolanda seemed to be making a pretty good living and had minimal debt.

I think that isn't completely unheard of in the beauty industry. She liked to shop and travel a lot but hey, what girl doesn't? Yolanda had lived in her apartment for about six months. She lived alone and casually dated. Her son did stay with her from time to time. I was going to have to find out her friends and boyfriends and try to get a read.

I wrote down all of the unknown numbers that kept appearing on Yolanda's phone records. I looked them up and basically did a background check. It would show phone numbers and addresses associated with anyone. It's not always completely up to date, but it's a good tool.

Yolanda was killed at about 5:00 a.m. The last phone call she'd received was from her son Qaw'mane.

Qaw'mane could definitely answer some of my questions if he ever returned my phone calls.

# CHAPTER 17

## SON OF A GUN

It was Monday, just after 11:00 p.m., and I was at my desk in Area Three when the phone rang. The building was quiet in that late-night way—dim hallways, humming vents, and detectives buried in paperwork they didn't want to finish. Officer Caroline Burgess, a uniformed patrol officer from the 11th District, was on the line. She said she had Yolanda's son Qaw'mane stopped on a traffic stop. Finally, some good news. My investigative alert had popped up on her squad car computer, also known as a PDT, the second she ran Qaw'mane's name. That alert was basically a stop order: if he encountered a Chicago police officer in any capacity, I would be notified and I would finally have a chance to talk to him, but only if he agreed.

I told Caroline to relocate him to Area Three, and apparently he was eager to talk to me as well. And now, after months of silence, he was sitting in the back of a squad car, headed straight to me.

John and I had spent the last few months trying everything, calling, texting, stopping by Qaw'mane's building on the West Side, the one that belonged to his grandfather. That's where we learned he'd foreclosed on the property, leaving his family blindsided. I pleaded with his relatives, asking them to help me track Yolanda's son down. Every lead was cold. Every attempt to reach him went straight to voicemail. It was like he'd fallen off the face of the earth on purpose.

So, I finally put the alert on him. At least then, if he got pulled over or filled out a case report somewhere in Chicago, I would know. I would be able to interview him or, at the very least, get a message to him that I needed him to call me.

That phone call from Officer Burgess changed everything.

When Qaw'mane arrived, we talked to him briefly in the hallway. Just small talk. He told us a little about his life like everything was normal, like we weren't investigating the murder of his mother. Then we escorted him into the interview room and told him to get comfortable. It was one of those dull rooms, concrete walls painted an ugly shade of off white, metal bench, a couple chairs that always felt colder than they needed to be. I've watched a lot of people fold in that exact room.

Once we got Qaw'mane settled, it didn't take long for the mask to slip. You could see the tension in his jaw, the nervous twitch of his hands. He was trying to act calm, trying to look unbothered, but the cracks were there, clear as day. His world was unraveling, and he knew it. What threw me wasn't what he admitted to; it was the way he delivered it. Like he'd been waiting for someone to pull the truth out of him.

"It was supposed to be a robbery," he said. His voice was strangely detached, almost emotionless, like he was describing someone else's life or a TV show he'd watched instead of his own mother's murder. That sentence was like a key turning in a locked door. My gut clenched. I knew this was just the surface. There was a whole iceberg under there, and the air in that room felt heavy and tight, like all of the ugly truth was pressing to get out. In that moment, Qaw'mane went from being the victim's grieving son to the person who had orchestrated her death.

We didn't have time to waste. We had forty-eight hours to keep him in custody before we either had to charge him or let him go. Forty-eight hours to piece this whole thing together, and once those hours were gone, so was our chance. So, we moved fast. From Qaw'mane's words, we followed every trail, every breadcrumb. We dug through phone records, studying call after call, trying to figure out who he was talking to. We combed through surveillance footage, rewinding and replaying until our eyes felt grainy. We followed the money too: bank withdrawals, things that only made sense if you were looking for something dark. And then there were the life insurance policies and hefty bank accounts stacked neatly, timed suspiciously, practically screaming motive. We'd already done all of the hard lifting. Now was the time to home in on the details.

And then he admitted everything. The dark figure entering his mother's building? That was his old neighbor, Eugene Spencer. Eugene lived in one of the apartments in his grandfather's building on the West Side. The trail didn't stop there. It led straight to Loriana Johnson, Qaw'mane's girlfriend and the getaway driver. Every step pointed toward one brutal truth: Yolanda Holmes, a woman who had given her son everything, had been betrayed by him in the cruelest way possible. From the inside out.

My sergeant ran out on the streets with Marco Garcia to look for Eugene Spencer. As luck would have it, he was homeless. So, there was no real address we could find him at. Thankfully, it was only a few days before Christmas, so we knew he would probably be going home to visit family. Turns out we were right. We contacted the guys from fugitive apprehension and asked them to help me find him. They followed a tip and caught him on the way to his family's house for Christmas.

Spencer didn't look surprised when we caught up to him. It was almost as if he expected it. He was placed in an interview room far away from Qaw'mane, so they couldn't talk to each other through the walls or give a "look" during a bathroom break. I walked into the interview room and un-cuffed him from the wall he was connected to.

I asked him if he needed anything.

He said he needed a napkin.

And I said okay for what.

He said his penis was leaking green stuff.

*Gross*, I thought. But if he was doing this to me because he thought this was going to stop me from trying to talk to him, he was wrong. This wasn't my first rodeo, nor was it my first impromptu penis conversation. So, I brought him a wet napkin.

John and I then came into the room and sat down with Spencer. Less than an hour in, he laid it all out in a full confession. No dancing around it. He briefly tried to minimize his involvement, but then he described meeting up with Qaw'mane in the basement of that foreclosed building on the West Side, the one that had belonged to Qaw'mane's grandfather. This wasn't some random attack. It was planned. Coordinated. Calculated. Cold.

"Here's the code," Qaw'mane told him as he provided Eugene with the code to his mom's apartment. "When my mom answers, cough and she'll think it's me."

And Eugene did exactly what he was told. There was only one problem: Curtis. Yolanda's boyfriend. No one knew he would be there. It was their fatal mistake. You don't leave a living witness behind, though I'm not too sure Eugene thought Curtis was still alive when he walked out of that building.

Curtis turned out to be our smoking gun, but only after dragging us through what felt like hours of pulling teeth. Eugene went on to tell us all of the little details that we could have never fathomed. Loriana had been in that basement meeting too, part of the plan from the start. Her job was simple: drive the getaway car. No questions. No hesitation.

Then came the part that still makes my stomach turn. Spencer described entering the apartment, shooting Yolanda while she slept, fighting with Curtis, and then returning to her bedroom to finish the job by stabbing her in the chest in her already dead body. She never had a chance.

And the worst part? Eugene was on the phone with Qaw'mane the whole time. Remember those ear buds we found on the scene? Qaw'mane was directing his own mother's murder like it was some sick video game.

"Turn left. Turn right."

And after the gunshots rang out—

"Make sure that bitch is dead," is what Qaw'mane ordered Eugene to do. Those words will forever stay with me. There are no words for what kind of person he is.

In that moment, I felt everything I'd trained for—the adrenaline, the calm, the anger, the sorrow. Because this wasn't just business. This was betrayal at its rawest. A son plotting matricide. Qaw'mane still believed he was going home. He proceeded to ask me how long he would be here. He then said he needed to use the restroom. You always have to be careful taking arrestees to use the restroom. This can be their only chance at escape.

I asked for two other detectives to assist me with escorting him to the bathroom. The prisoner bathroom is reminiscent of the first lockup I ever saw in Terry, Montana. There's no sink, just a toilet. It's disgusting, but the sinks were removed after a prisoner drank bleach during a futile attempt to kill himself. He didn't die, but what a horrible way to try to die had he succeeded. He ended up really sick. If I accidentally drank something that had touched bleach, I would probably keel over and die. This guy drank it like a Gatorade and other than a stomach ache and vomiting, he was fine. After that fiasco, they decided to get rid of all of the cleaning supplies and access to sinks.

We offered Qaw'mane some sanitizer and hand wipes and led him back to his interview room. We gave him a mattress to lie on and proceeded to ask him if he was hungry. He said he was starving, so one of the other guys headed out to get him some McDonalds.

I decided to go outside to clear my mind. I walked down out through the rear exit that we aren't supposed to use. It's actually supposed to be secure, but it's always left open for the smokers. Luckily, we have so many smokers that the exit is never unsecured because someone is always there smoking. I went down a flight of stairs, walked outside, and was almost blinded. I realized it was already after 7:00 a.m. and the sun was coming out. The sun felt good up against my face, and it was still eerily quiet.

It was like the few quiet moments before everyone wakes up. Any minute, normal people would begin the hustle and bustle of their day. The locals would be out walking their dogs soon. The runners were currently lacing up their shoes and drinking their first cup of coffee while getting prepared for their morning run while Qaw'mane sat in a small, eight-by-ten-foot room, wondering what his fate will be.

I always wonder how I would fare in a regular job. Like a nine to five, complete with those after work happy hours that I hear so much about. I know that was never really the life for me. But sometimes, when I'm at work for days upon days, I wonder who I would be if I'd taken another route in life.

After hours of interviews and watching and re-watching videos, I was tired and the only thing I could think about was sleep. I decided to go back upstairs and talk to Qaw'mane one more time before I drove home to take a nap.

I got in the car and sat there for a second before I turned the radio on and listened to some country music on the way home. This was a futile attempt to turn my brain off for a bit. I realized there was no way I was going to have the patience or concentration to finish this investigation if I didn't get a nap in.

After my nap, I was rested and ready to dive back in. It was Christmas time, and all of the red lights were twinkling in the area, except these weren't the kind you would expect. These red lights were the notification that the electronic recording interrogation was officially in session.

John, Art, Marco, Greg, and I went full force, methodically tearing apart every angle, leaving no stone unturned. Piece by piece, we got the full story. What had started as a twisted, selfish plan by a son who thought he could have it all—fame, fortune, everything—had spiraled out of control. His so-called "trusted companions" turned on Qaw'mane just as quickly as he'd turned on them. Classic. It was the kind of betrayal that never surprised me but still stung, every time.

We sealed the case, called the State's Attorney's office, and requested charges for first-degree murder on all three of them. And just like that, the charges were approved. The outcome we'd hoped for was finally within reach. All of the long hours, the sleepless nights, the digging through phone records, the late-night interrogations had finally paid off. The case was closed, and we'd secured justice for Yolanda.

And with that, we closed the book. Qaw'mane was eventually convicted of first-degree murder, home invasion, and everything else that came with orchestrating his own mother's death. Ninety-nine years in prison was his sentence, practically a lifetime for every year she raised him. Eugene Spencer—the so-called "friend," the muscle Qaw'mane had sent to do his dirty work—got one hundred years. A century. That kind of sentence makes the point clear: you're never stepping foot outside again.

Loriana Johnson, the getaway driver, was the only one who took the stand. She pled guilty to a lesser charge and cut her deal, and she followed through. She testified against Qaw'mane and Spencer in open court and walked the entire room through what had happened, her voice shaking but steady enough to hold. She told the jury what she'd seen, what she'd heard, and what she'd helped them do. Her testimony locked the whole case in place.

But here's the part that people don't understand, the part that never makes sense from the outside. Even cooperating, even after taking her plea, even after admitting what she'd done, Loriana still stayed loyal to Qaw'mane in her own twisted way. She wasn't testifying because she'd suddenly grown a conscience or because she wanted justice for Yolanda. She testified because she had no choice. It was survival.

Her loyalty to him ran deeper than the facts, deeper than the courtroom, deeper than the crime itself. The girl tattooed his name on her groin while she was awaiting trial. Let that sink in. Facing years in prison, knowing the weight of the charges, knowing the police had her dead to rights, she still marked herself with his name in one of the most intimate places a person can. That's not love. That's not devotion. That's brainwashing mixed with fear mixed with whatever strange power he had over her. It was disturbing and sad but honestly, predictable.

None of the guys testified, but each of them tried to save his own ass. They didn't have loyalty to each other, only to themselves. By the time the trial came around, the house of cards had collapsed, and they all knew it. Loriana told the truth because it was the only way for her to crawl out from under the mess Qaw'mane had dragged her into. Spencer didn't say a word. And Qaw'mane? He opted not to testify. But he strutted through court with sadness on his face like he was still performing, like the courtroom was just another stage and he was the headliner.

The verdicts came down hard, the sentences even harder. And after the last piece of paperwork was signed and the last door clanged shut behind them, the chapter was done.

But cases like this don't really end. They sit with you. They remind you what people are capable of, how far selfishness can reach, how deep manipulation can cut, and

how loyalty, when twisted the wrong way, can ruin entire
lives.

# CHAPTER 18

# I'VE BEEN WAITING FOR YOU

On the way home, I decided to stop at the grocery store to grab a few things. I was tired in that way only detectives understand, the kind of tiredness that settles into your bones, but I was looking forward to a glass of wine and reruns of *Law & Order* with the pugs. They wouldn't judge me for drinking alone.

When I left the office, I found a thick stack of supplemental reports stuffed into my mailbox: follow-ups from patrol, phone records finally logged, a couple late interviews typed up by detectives who somehow manage to write like they're being chased. Nothing urgent, nothing explosive, but enough to tell me that I needed a break.

I tucked the pile under my arm, intending to skim through it when I got home. *Just a few pages*, I told myself. *Just enough to clear the plate.* But that's how it always starts. A few pages turns into sixty, and before you know it, you're cross-referencing timestamps at midnight and talking to the dog like he can give you legal advice.

I was walking to my car reading the top page when that familiar chill hit me, the hair on the back of my neck standing straight up. Instinct. The old sixth sense that whispers, *Pay attention,* even when everything looks normal. I stopped walking. Lowered the paperwork. Turned and scanned the lot.

The place was darker than usual, like half of the overhead lights had called in sick. The shadows looked heavy and deliberate, pooled in corners where they didn't usually sit. The whole world sounded muffled: the low hum of the highway, a car radio blaring something I couldn't make out, a dog barking somewhere far off like it was warning someone I couldn't see.

It was the kind of silence you only notice because something is wrong inside it. That's when it hit me. This night wasn't done with me yet. And whatever was waiting, it wasn't in the reports.

I fumbled for my phone, not because I wanted to scroll but because it makes light; the screen threw a little bit of light across the asphalt and for a second, that was enough to pretend I wasn't alone.

Then a voice… the kind of male voice that I should have catalogued earlier: familiar, too casual for the hour.

"Hey, Detective." And a hand on my shoulder, warm, greasy, the whole shock of it. I jumped. He jumped. We were both startled like we'd been set to a trigger.

I turned around and the world narrowed. Two cars towed into the lot blocked my view and created a large shadow. There, a couple feet behind me, a man stood half in the light, half in the dark, as if he was trying to decide which to choose. He was small, White, disheveled—the kind of person who looks like the city chewed him up and spit him out at me.

He reached out like he was about to offer his hand to shake, like this was a friendly meeting. That gesture alone should have told him something: I don't shake hands. I wash my hands a hundred times a day—not for politeness, but for the things hands pick up in a hospital room or a crime scene—and I wasn't about to find out what kinds of things this man had been touching.

Before I could seize his face, I smelled him. It came in a wave: uncut, acidic. Face unshaven, oily skin that hadn't met soap in days, hair with that stale, sour tang of someone who sleeps in his clothes.

Under it all was something worse—urine, the dry, sharp smell that sticks in the back of your throat and tells you this person hasn't been inside a bathroom with hot water in a long time. The smell made my stomach turn. I stepped back and reached for my gun with my left hand. The movement was automatic, everything I'd trained into my body over years of experience with bad people. The weight of the holster on my hip gave me a sense of comfort and confidence.

He said, "Hey. You don't remember me? You saved my life."

My heart was beating in my ears because he basically followed me to my car. I couldn't believe I'd let him get close enough to touch me. I couldn't believe I hadn't heard him coming. For a second, I was furious with myself, the way you are when you know you should have seen it coming and didn't. Then the anger clicked over like a switch into something harder.

"No, I don't." I let the words hang in the cold. My voice did what it always does on high alert. It went flat, controlled… almost too calm.

"You have about thirty seconds," I told him. It wasn't a joke. It wasn't a threat for theatrics. It was a fair warning.

His hands went up like he was an actor who had finally learned his cue. He edged back a little, but not far enough.

"My name's Jimmy," he said. "You saved me." The words tumbled out like he'd rehearsed these lines in front of the mirror several times and decided tonight was the night to deliver them.

As the streetlight swung across his face, I could actually see him—the crooked split of his lip, the hollow under his cheekbones, and the emptiness in his eyes.

A police memory clicked loose: he'd come into my station several years back, right after he'd been released from Statesville. He was supposed to register as a sex offender within three days of his release from the Illinois Department of Corrections. I figured out he was one of those people who don't understand the rules or are too stubborn or too dumb to follow them. In Illinois, you must register within seventy-two hours if you've been convicted of a sex crime. Not at a satellite station. Not at the nearest police station desk. You go to headquarters, bankers' hours, Monday through Friday.

When he first came in, the desk officers called the Detective Division for assistance. They had no idea where he was supposed to go to register. They assumed we, the detectives, would know where to send him. So, it wasn't my job, but I decided to assist them and ran downstairs to talk to him and try to send him in the right direction. I used my discretion. Instead of hauling him straight back into custody for failing to register, I told him where to go and how to do it. I read his criminal history upstairs and found what I didn't want to find—a conviction for criminal sexual assault. The victim was a seven-year-old. The more I thought about it, the more my stomach turned. That's when the "I should have arrested you" voice in my head started crowding the room.

Jimmy was babbling now, insisting I'd rescued him. He said I was an angel when I arrested him—except he was confused, I didn't arrest him. I tucked that away for a second and then had to figure out what to do with the man who'd been waiting for me all day. It's one thing to have a guy leave you a message at the office; it's another thing entirely for him to sit in a parking lot at 1:00 a.m. and wait for you. The math in my head was ugly: time, motive, opportunity. Stalking behavior.

"I never arrested you, and you're definitely confused about what you think you remember," I told him.

My grip was on the gun but my eyes were measuring everything else: the way his hands trembled, the rhythm of his breathing, the clench in his jaw.

He began to cry… and I don't mean a quiet catching of breath; I mean full-on blubbering. It was the voice of a creep who was a young child's nightmare.

"Please," he begged. "I couldn't reach you. I had to come. I wanted to thank you." He reached for a smaller truth, the one that made him look repentant or broken, like he thought that would make me soft.

I hate rapists. Of course, I hate them like the rest of the world does, only my job gives the hate new dimensions: paperwork, subpoenas, child victims, court dates where people try to explain away what's not explainable. But I also have to be smart enough to see the theater and stupid enough to not fall into it. If I wasn't a cop, the answer in me would be immediate and ugly.

I pictured what I would like to do, but I liked my job and my freedom. Instead, I had to handle a human being who was presently both pathetic and dangerous.

"Get out of here," I told him. It came out low. I considered calling it in, trading my gun for my phone and dialing 911, but that would have meant taking my eyes off him for a second too long. While I was hesitating, he flooded the quiet with more nonsense: that he wanted to pay for his sins, that I was beautiful to him, that I'd done him a favor by arresting him—all untrue and all vomitus in the same beat.

And then, uncertain as angels are these days, a figure dropped into the world beside us like a shadow stepped off the curb: Sergeant Bob appeared as if he'd been in the air and someone turned on a light. One second it's me and this tragic, greasy man; the next second, Bob's there. He moved like a man who had worked too many midnight parking lot calls; his cuff hand was out and the sex offender barely had a moment to register that the party was over. Bob popped on handcuffs with one quick, efficient motion I'd seen a thousand times. It was the motion of someone who knows how to cut scenes into pieces and throw them away.

"Get out of here, kid," he said, and the word "kid" made the whole thing smaller and more ridiculous than Jimmy clearly was. I didn't argue. I didn't check to see what happened after I heard the click of steel. I didn't turn around to make sure Jimmy got hauled off. I knew by the cadence in Bob's voice that whatever theater Jimmy had planned was concluded.

I walked to my car with my boots making a loud *click clock* sound on the oil-stained pavement. The light from my phone stuttered off puddles; the scent of exhaust and that lingering human stink trailed behind me, like a shadow that won't stop whispering. I slid into the driver's seat and didn't breathe out until the engine was growling and the taillights were a red memory in the rearview mirror.

They don't call me "Lead Foot" for nothing. I put that creep behind me fast. I wasn't running, just purposefully getting home with the knowledge that I didn't have to look back. In the rearview, the parking lot shrank until it was only a blotch of dark. I replayed it in my head, of course, like every detective does. The jump, the hand, the smell, the thing that made me reach for my gun instead of my phone. The stupid part of me that scolded myself for not seeing him sooner. The other part of me that was glad my rule— no handshakes, wash your hands—had been in place long enough to keep me from something worse.

That night I slept badly, because you never quite stop seeing the thing that could have gone wrong. But I slept knowing two things: one, that my training worked when my instincts were rattled; and two, that being "nice" on the job carries its own cost. You can be kind and still be dangerous. You can give directions instead of cuffs and still keep a hand near your holster. You can do the right thing for the right reason and still have to live with the part of you that wonders if you did enough.

When you work in this world, the city deposits certain souvenirs into your skin: smells that stick, voices you can't unhear, faces that show up in the dark. That night, the souvenir was a greasy handprint on my shoulder in a parking lot that smelled like urine and oil and bad endings. It was a reminder that being a detective isn't glamor, it's proximity. Proximity to what people do when they want to hurt, and proximity to the colleagues who step out of nowhere and put things back in order. It's why you drive like hell to get away, and why you keep washing your hands long after the scene is gone.

Somewhere in the middle of grizzly homicide investigations and bikini competitions, I somehow managed to land one of the most unexpected opportunities of my life. I was lucky enough to get cast in a Dick Wolf television show called *Dead Again.* It all started in a way that still feels surreal. The producers somehow got a hold of a press conference John and I had done after solving a real "heater" case in the Lincoln Park neighborhood. That case would end up being one of the most talked-about in the city.

It was a senseless one. Sally Katona-King, a beloved deacon of the Evangelical Lutheran Church, had been making her way home in March 2011 when everything went wrong. She was walking down the metal stairs at the Fullerton Red Line station when Prince Watson, the seventeen-year-old offender, was fleeing from a robbery on the CTA train. In his haste, he plowed into Sally with such force that he sent her petite body tumbling down the stairs, ripping her aorta right out of its chamber. The woman, who had given so much to the community, died in a matter of moments. This case wasn't just a tragedy—it was also one of the first patterns of iPhone robberies that were spreading across the Red Line.

John and I worked that case alongside Sheryl and Jude, two of the most respected veteran detectives I'd ever known. Together, we pieced together the puzzle. It was like chasing shadows in the dark, but we got lucky. We caught the offender and, to our surprise, he actually gave a full confession. It was rare. So many of the cases we worked on had offenders who would lie through their teeth, but this one, Prince Watson, seemed to carry some real remorse.

As always, it was the same story. He was a young man from a broken home, with no means of income, and a criminal background to boot. He was just trying to make quick money. That quick money that cost an innocent woman her life. It was another brutal reminder that crime doesn't just affect the victim. It destroys everyone it touches, including the person committing the crime.

So, after we wrapped the case, John and I went downstairs for the press conference, which was being held by Commander Gary Yamashiroya of Area Three. I had no idea what I was about to walk into. In a strange twist of fate, during the conference, Commander Yamashiroya looked over and said, "You know what? Michele, why don't you come down here and tell them what happened?" And just like that, I was thrust into my first-ever press conference, completely unprepared.

I'd never spoken to the press before. I was used to solving crimes, not standing in front of cameras and microphones. But as nervous as I was, I stood up, walked down, and did my best to explain the case. And to my surprise? It went pretty damn well. I didn't fumble my words. I didn't choke. I actually held my ground. It felt good—too good, in fact.

While I was still knee-deep in real homicide cases, I started taking days off here and there to fly to New York— or wherever I was needed—to film the episodes of *Dead Again.* It was exhausting, sure. But it was also exhilarating. The adrenaline rush of switching between the world of real crime scenes and the world of reality TV was like nothing I'd ever experienced before. I didn't sleep at all, but that was fine by me. I thrived on the chaos, on the pace of it all. Every moment, every challenge, every shift between the two worlds only made me feel more alive. I never imagined that

I would end up here, juggling real murder investigations and the world of television… but somehow, in the most unlikely of ways, I was. And honestly? I wouldn't have changed a thing.

# CHAPTER 19

## SOLO ON AN AIRPLANE

In police work, timing is everything, and luck—real, stupid, unpredictable luck—is the secret ingredient behind almost every good investigation. People talk about instincts like they're some mystical sixth sense, but half of the time it's luck nudging you in the ribs and the other half is you trusting that tiny voice in your head saying, *Turn left, not right.*

There's a theory I've come to believe, mostly because I've lived it: when you're running late, when everything is falling apart, when the universe seems to be throwing roadblocks in your path like some cosmic traffic cop, sometimes that's not bad luck. Sometimes that's the universe yanking you out of the way of something darker. Something waiting just around the corner. A warning disguised as inconvenience. But I didn't fully believe that back in March of 2016. Not yet.

That evening, while most of the city was heading home from a long day of work or enjoying happy hour with co-workers and friends, Soldon Armstrong was walking down the West Side of Chicago near Jackson and Pulaski. It's a loud, restless stretch of the city—buses hissing as they kneel at the curb, horns blaring in impatient bursts, people shouting from open car windows like the street itself is part of the conversation. Nothing ever really feels still. Open-air drug markets blend into the background, operating in plain sight, as ordinary as traffic lights. So do the open-air cigarette markets.

Maybe it's something uniquely Chicago, but in addition to dope spots, we also have loosey spots, pronounced like the name Lucy, where individual cigarettes are sold one at a time by street vendors posted up on the corners. These places draw foot traffic, cash exchanges, and attention, and with that comes opportunity. Not just for hustling, but for crime. The lines between routine and risk can blur pretty fast.

Jackson and Pulaski is the kind of intersection where you learn early to keep your head on a swivel. You read faces without staring, clock movement without reacting, and stay aware of who's behind you even when you're walking forward. Soldon didn't do that. Or maybe he did and decided it didn't matter. Maybe he thought the rules didn't apply to him. Maybe he thought he was untouchable.

A group of younger guys from the neighborhood spotted him. And believe me, he's pretty hard to miss. He's built like a linebacker, a brick wall with a neck to match. They'd been hunting for him, looking to settle a debt Soldon had racked up, one he apparently had no intention of paying. There's no polite way to say it: these guys weren't out for a friendly conversation. They were out to embarrass him, scare him, and maybe rough him up. Who knows? That's the danger of street logic: once it starts, it doesn't have brakes.

They tried to bait him into a verbal fight right there on the sidewalk. But Soldon was the wrong guy to try that with. Wrong temperament, wrong personality, wrong history. Soldon was a convicted murderer who had already spent years in prison, so this sneak attack was probably the wrong plan. This incident was captured on video. It's the type of scene that makes your stomach clench because you can sense disaster moving in, slow and deliberate, like a fog rolling across asphalt.

Fredrick Brown was the first to step up to Soldon, the one who actually put hands on him right in the middle of the street... In seconds, the argument turned into a full-blown fight that rolled onto the sidewalk right near the bus stop shelter located on the corner. Shoving. Fists. A crowd forming, the way crowds always do when blood is on the horizon.

And then Soldon reached inside his jacket. The knife he pulled out wasn't a pocketknife. It wasn't some cheap folding thing you buy at a gas station. This was a hunting knife, a blade long enough to make your heart drop. He swung once, a brutal, decisive motion, and stabbed Fredrick so deep the blade nearly came out his back.

The crowd scattered. Fredrick collapsed. People screamed.

He didn't make it. Doctors officially called it at the hospital, but the truth is, Fredrick died right there on the pavement before the ambulance even cleared the corner.

By the time we arrived on scene, most of the witnesses had disappeared and the ones who were there had selective amnesia or they hadn't been looking in that direction when the stabbing occurred. We searched the area in hopes of finding the discarded murder weapon but never found it. Lucky for us, the liquor store located on the corner was equipped with pretty good surveillance cameras that captured most of the incident. I talked to the cashier/security guard Justin, whom I should have recruited for the Chicago Police Department. He was sharp, confident, and well put together. He deserved to work somewhere better than a shitty liquor store on a corner. It was far too dangerous and regardless of what they were paying him, it wasn't enough. I keep meaning to see what he's up to lately.

From the beginning, the name "Solo" kept coming up. Over and over again. If you knew Solo, you would know why.

I met Fredrick's mother later that week. She told me she had little faith in the justice system and not just because her son was gone, but because *her mother* had been murdered years ago in Arizona and her killer was never caught. Three generations of pain folded into one woman. And she was supposed to trust us to get it right. That's a heavy thing to look someone in the eye and promise.

Soldon, whom we would eventually come to know as "Solo," ran. Not north. Not south. He fled the entire Midwest and somehow ended up living on an Indian reservation in Connecticut after meeting a girl named Morning Star at the local Walmart. That part is still wild to me. You can plan every escape route, you can craft every alibi, but life has a sense of humor, and apparently Solo's destiny involved aisle nine and someone named Morning Star.

John and I were hot on Solo's trail. We secured a warrant for his arrest, packed it with every detail we could, and hoped it would be enough to put him in cuffs if anyone caught even a hint of him.

Months passed before we got the call: Solo had been picked up by U.S. Marshals outside the reservation. He was being held in Connecticut, waiting for extradition back to Chicago. That was the moment everything kicked into gear.

John and I started planning the trip, booking the flights, grabbing the case file, reviewing every witness statement. We notified the State's Attorney's office so they could send a prosecutor with us. We had to "lock in" the witnesses once we got there. Lock in meant we would take their statements, put everything on video or handwriting, and seal it tight so nobody could wiggle out of it later. We thought this was just a routine transport. A simple grab-the-guy, sign-the-papers, bring-him-home kind of trip. But we were wrong.

This case was about to twist into something none of us could have predicted, something that would change every one of our lives.

Most of it sounds unbelievable, but every single part is true. So, John and I started planning our big adventure to Connecticut, which sounds glamorous until you remember we're cops and nothing we do is actually glamorous. We quickly found out there were zero nonstop flights from Chicago to wherever the hell in Connecticut we needed to go. Connecticut apparently missed the memo about being a real state with real airports. Armstrong was apparently in jail somewhere near Foxwood Casino, which I'd heard great things about.

So we figured, fine—fly into a big airport instead. New York City, it is. The upside? We could get there early and do a little recon. And by "recon," I obviously mean: eat good food, people-watch, and pretend we're on a work trip for the FBI instead of dealing with a guy named Soldon who stabbed someone to death over a little fight.

The extradition officer assigned to us was a guy named Officer Joseph Tripoli. Salt-of-the-earth type. No nonsense. I told Joe, completely joking, that I only stayed in five-star hotels in the middle of Times Square. I said it with my straightest detective face.

Joe paused. "We, uh… can't do that. There are budgets."

I told him to do his best because I only insisted on the best. John and I also needed separate rooms and preferably on opposite wings of the hotel so we could have "privacy." Maria Augustus, the State's Attorney, was coming with us. She played along with our demands. Maria is a mad genius, emphasis on mad. She's brash, abrasive, tells it like it is, and swears more than I do. She's got long, wild, dark curls and hates almost everyone. John and I both love Maria, and we were ecstatic that she was coming with us on our extradition.

***

I was fully expecting Joe to put us in some depressing airport hotel in Queens, where the highlight was a broken ice machine and the smell of old carpet. But somehow… somehow, Joe actually came through. He booked us a legitimately cool hotel smack in the middle of Times Square.

Neon chaos, tourists, street performers, the whole circus. I was shocked, impressed, and slightly disappointed that my joke had worked.

But then, of course, life laughed in my face.

John called me in a panic. His wife was nine months pregnant and basically a sneeze away from giving birth. So, at the last minute, he had to cancel. I got it, but I still groaned loudly and dramatically because I'm petty like that.

Enter Detective Marco Garcia. Marco cleared his schedule without hesitation, which immediately made me suspicious because cops never clear their schedule unless they're trying to avoid something at home.

Maria was coming too, so we had a full crew. And to make the trip slightly more tolerable, I planned to meet up with a friend of mine out there, Steph Watts, a TV producer I'd worked with on one of the true crime TV shows I was on. I figured if we were going to be extraditing someone across state lines, we could at least squeeze one moment of fun out of this depressing line of work.

We got to NYC early enough to drop our bags and hunt down food. The hotel had a Greek restaurant inside, which I immediately vetoed. No more Greek food. John ate at Greek restaurants every day of his life like it was some kind of religion, and I was over it. So, we asked the concierge for a recommendation, and she told us to go to the "Irish pub down the street." We walked outside and immediately saw two Irish pubs, one on each side of the street. Classic New York. We picked the one on the left because it looked livelier and didn't smell like stale Guinness from the doorway.

We sat down, started looking at menus, and I caught Marco staring off into space like he'd seen a ghost or had suddenly realized he left his stove on at home. I followed his line of sight and boom! There it was.

His wife.

Walking down the sidewalk.

With her boyfriend.

What. Are. The. Chances?

Seriously, what are the odds of your cheating spouse strolling past your random Irish pub in New York City while you're on a last-minute work trip you weren't even originally supposed to be on? The odds are probably, like, ten million to one. Maybe more. Maybe divine intervention. Maybe karma. Maybe just really dark cosmic comedy.

The look on her face said everything: busted.

Marco excused himself with the kind of forced calm that tells you he's either about to cry or put someone through a wall. Maria and I exchanged a look, shrugged, and went back to our drinks. What else could we do? We'd both seen enough relationship disasters to know when to stay out of it.

The next morning, Marco showed up like nothing had happened. Zero details. Zero conversation. Face like a stone wall. And honestly? Fine by me. I wasn't trying to play therapist on a day when we had to go collect a fugitive with a knife fetish.

We took the long drive to Connecticut, passing endless trees, quiet towns, and the kind of gas stations that make you check your back seat twice. We interviewed Soldon, who was now going by "Solo," because of course he was, and he was exactly as charming as you would expect a guy hiding out on a reservation with a girl he'd met in Walmart to be.

After the interviews and paperwork, we took Solo— quiet, cuffed, and suddenly very cooperative—back on the long road toward LaGuardia. Then we boarded a plane with him like it was the most normal thing in the world. Just another day in homicide.

The road trip from Connecticut to LaGuardia felt more like a bizarre buddy comedy than a prisoner transport. At some point, we slipped into quoting *Coming to America*, trading lines back and forth like we were just ordinary people killing time on the highway instead of two detectives and a prosecutor escorting a convicted killer. And honestly? Soldon could have passed for a used-car salesman instead of a felon. He was sharp, funny, quick with a comeback, and had that weird gift of making you feel like he was in on the same joke you were. He didn't seem like someone who had taken a life… well, actually, two lives so far.

On the drive he told us his story, and I learned why he'd already served time as a convicted murderer years before we arrested him on this case. It wasn't some cold-blooded murder plot, it was a robbery gone wrong. Someone died, and that death sat on him whether he'd meant for it to happen or not. He didn't actually pull the trigger, I might add. Not exactly the monster the paperwork made him out to be. Still, I wasn't stupid. Charming or not, he was still a man in shackles, and I never let myself forget that.

By the time we got to the airport, the reality of the situation came crashing back. We had to put him in a wheelchair and drape a poncho over him to hide the cuffs and minimize the stares from other travelers. The whole setup felt ridiculous, like we were sneaking a celebrity through a back entrance instead of rolling a convicted felon up to the gate.

The flight was uneventful aside from the fact that Solo had to pee every fifteen minutes, which meant we had to escort him each time. He also had quite an appetite and used both of our per diems and his own per diem buying him snacks and food.

The flight attendants were **supposed** to let us deplane last, quietly, discreetly. Of course, that didn't happen. Quite the opposite. They must have taken one look at us and panicked, because instead of a subtle, "Let the law enforcement officers exit first," they got on the PA system and announced, loud enough for every passenger to hear, that everyone needed to stay seated while "special passengers" were taken off the plane. So subtle.

When we finally stood up and started moving, I could feel the eyes boring into us. I'm pretty sure we ruined a few vacations the moment Soldon limped down the aisle, shackles clinking under the poncho, flanked by two armed detectives who definitely did **not** look like part of the in-flight entertainment. People gasped. One woman covered her kid's eyes. Another guy clutched his neck pillow like a shield. And there we were, just doing our job, escorting the "killer who didn't feel like a killer" off a commercial flight like it was just another Tuesday.

Solo ended up getting charged with first-degree murder. A few years later, after the State's Attorneys talked it over with Fredrick's family, they agreed to let Solo plead guilty to second-degree murder, mostly because there was a real chance he would beat the case at trial, and with his prior conviction, he was also risking the possibility of life without parole if he lost. In the end, Solo went to prison. And honestly? I'm sure he's over there doing what he always does, winning everyone over, like jail is just another stage he's performing on.

In 2022, in a strange and cruel twist of fate, Joe Tripoli—the detective who helped us coordinate Soldon's extradition—died from COVID. His death was a sobering reminder of how little control any of us really have, no matter how much we like to believe otherwise

# CHAPTER 20

# THE ROADS I NEVER PLANNED TO TAKE

I didn't take the traditional route that most women map out for themselves. Honestly, nothing about my life followed any kind of script. I never had the white picket fence plan, the sorority engagement photos, or the bridal shower registry full of monogrammed towels. I was too busy choosing a career where monogrammed anything gets covered in blood, glass, or gunshot residue. And then, I got on the police department.

At some point, I tried the whole find-a-nice-normal-guy thing. In my case, that meant another cop. Everyone tells you to avoid that. Every older woman on this job grabs your arm in the bathroom at roll call and whispers, "Honey, don't date on the job." But who else are you going to meet when you work nights, live on caffeine and trauma, and your entire social circle consists of other cops, a couple of ER nurses, and the occasional bartender who knows your order before you sit down? So yes, I married a cop. I'll call him Mr. Nice Guy. I tried to do it "right." Marriage, maybe kids, maybe that calm life I saw other women building like it was nothing. But my life doesn't do calm, and it sure as hell doesn't do easy.

When that marriage blew up after seven years, it felt like someone had taken a blowtorch to whatever structure

I thought I was building. And then the clock started ticking louder. Each year that passed, the idea of having kids felt like it was drifting further away. And when you're a woman in law enforcement, no one really talks about that. You're out there kicking down doors and running homicide scenes, while quietly wondering if you missed your only window to build a family of your own.

A lot of cops end up alone. It's one of the saddest truths of this job. The divorce rate is high, the burnout rate is higher, and too many officers retire with nothing to live for except a pension, a recliner, and whatever memories haven't been swallowed by trauma. When the job goes away, a lot of people lose their identity. You retire that badge and suddenly, you're just… a regular person. And you don't know how to be that.

I've asked myself the same questions: What am I if I'm not the police? If the crime scenes don't call my name, do I even exist? Does anyone care about me? Do *I* care about me?

This job warps you. We live in suspicion. We don't trust anyone. Motives, stories, emotions… everything gets filtered through a homicide detective's mind. And yet somehow, when the truth is right in your own bed, you miss it. Or maybe you don't miss it; you just refuse to look because if you acknowledge it, your entire world shifts.

I had all of the signs that my husband was seeking extracurricular activities. All. Of. The. Signs. I ignored them, not because I was stupid, but because I wanted to believe I was special. That I was so amazing he wouldn't dare do that to me. But betrayal doesn't care how amazing you are. It comes anyway. And when it does, the fall is brutal. There are moments, especially now—older, wiser, scarred both physically and emotionally—when I feel like I'm only a few steps away from impending disaster… or becoming a full-blown cat lady. Or dog lady. And honestly? I'm not even mad about it. But long before that happy ending, there is the department and the unspoken rules women navigate from day one.

Here's the truth: there are so few women in the department that when you first get on, you suddenly feel like a supermodel. You could look like you just rolled out of a dumpster, and someone will still tell you you're beautiful. It boosts your ego... and becomes a trap.

Because policing has a double standard no one wants to own up to. A woman dates a couple guys on the job and she's instantly "that girl." The whispers start. The judgment follows. You don't just get rumors, you get a reputation. It sticks longer than gunshot residue and is ten times harder to wash off. Meanwhile, a male cop can sleep with half of the district and he's a legend. High-fives at lineup. War stories. "Atta boy." Boys being boys. Same behavior. Completely different consequences.

In this job, one rumor can erase a hundred good arrests. One whisper can overshadow years of hard work. So, women learn to walk a tightrope. You try to be twice as sharp, twice as tough, and twice as careful. You can be the best detective in the room, but people will always remember the story someone told about you before they remember the case you solved.

So yes: dating a coworker? Usually a bad idea. But for women cops, the dating pool is basically (1) other cops, or (2) firemen. And guess what? Option two isn't the magical solution people think it is.

Firemen are America's heroes. They have calendars. We have body cams. They save cats from trees. We get called racists in Comment sections by people who don't even know our names. And yet women love them. Firemen are hot. Big muscles. Good hair. They work eighty-something days a year, so they've got time to work on their bodies... and other things. You know that saying about idle minds being the devil's workshop? Firehouses could be the case study.

So, when you're a woman in law enforcement, your love life becomes this weird combination of limited options, unfair expectations, and the constant fear that one wrong move will follow you your entire career. And meanwhile, you're trying to solve murders, stay alive, and maybe find someone who doesn't crumble at the idea of dating a woman in power.

Those men, the ones not threatened by you, not intimidated by your job, not looking to compete? Those men are rare. Not lottery rare. More like a meteor hitting your back yard rare.

But in the end, I did find one good one… just much later in life, after I'd rebuilt myself from the ground up. After betrayal, after heartbreak, after I thought motherhood might never happen. After I'd already earned my stripes, my scars, and my place in this job.

My life didn't follow the traditional route.

Thank God.

Because the route I ended up on made me the woman I am today.

# CHAPTER 21

# WARNING LABELS DON'T STOP BULLETS

At one point in my life, I was solving murders in real alleys by day and re-investigating controversial homicide cases on national television by night. The filming on the TV show *Dead Again* took longer than expected. They decided to change up the format of the last episode, which took me to the Allan B. Polunsky Unit death row facility in Texas to interview convicted killer Rodney Reed. That interview was intense and the first and only trip I ever made to death row.

So, my TV homicide cases took a turn into reality when I was set to interview Rodney a few days before his planned execution early in 2015. On paper, it sounded surreal. In reality, it was even stranger. On my days off… what few I had… I would fly to New York City and Bastrop, Texas and then fly right back to Chicago to work my actual cases. The production was kind enough to build the filming schedule around my real job, which meant I went six months without a single day off. And spoiler… Rodney got a last minute stay of execution.

The irony wasn't lost on me. On television, I was re-investigating controversial cold cases, walking through evidence with a camera crew, breaking things down for the audience. It felt like an extension of my job except this time, someone was doing my hair and makeup, and there were lights instead of squad cars. I would solve cases on TV, then come home and solve them for real.

My sergeant noticed. While I was playing detective on screen, he was handing me some of the hardest cases off camera. Bodies found in alleys. No witnesses. No cameras. No help. The kind of cases that don't make for good television but make for long nights and longer reports. It wasn't punishment exactly, but it also wasn't a coincidence.

I'd earned those cases.

I was exhausted, wired, and running on adrenaline. I would be standing on a set one day, explaining evidence to a national audience, and standing over a body the next, knowing no amount of lighting or editing was going to make this one palatable. It blurred everything—work, fear, ambition, anxiety. The signs on the doors felt more ridiculous than ever. The guns felt heavier. The responsibility felt louder. Somewhere in between all of that, people were asking me if a sign on a door could stop a bullet.

This wasn't my first TV gig, though it was definitely the most exciting. In 2008, years before *Dead Again,* I was offered an incredible opportunity to work with psychic Allison Dubois on a TV pilot called *Soul Evidence.* Allison had inspired the main character in the TV show *Medium,* which played from 2005 to 2011. I flew out to Garden Grove, California, to re-investigate the rape and murder of nineteen-year-old nursing student Janet Stallcup, an unsolved case from 1976. While filming the pilot, Allison and I connected well; she thought like a cop, which made our partnership exciting. Unfortunately, the show wasn't picked up, and the main critique was that I didn't come off as believable in my role as a homicide detective. I couldn't help but feel frustrated. How could they not see that I was a real detective living this reality?

Fast forward about a year later, to 2009, and my lieutenant randomly approached me with an odd request.

"Hey, do you want to do a buccal swab for some detectives in California for an old case from the 1980s?" Knowing I loved California, he thought maybe I would be summoned to California for court at some point. I jumped at the chance and called the detective, only to find out it was for the Garden Grove Police Department and the Janet Stallcup case. What were the odds? I couldn't believe it. The detectives were aware of my involvement in the *Soul Evidence* pilot and asked, "Wait, are you the actress from the TV show that was out here?"

I gulped and quickly clarified, "I'm not an actress; I'm a detective."

The case led us to a suspect who had moved to Chicago. My partner John and I met him at his expensive Lakeview home, where he was oddly excited to show his kids what was going on. We awkwardly explained to his kids that "Daddy is a suspect in a murder," trying to strike a balance between our serious investigation and the interesting family dynamic.

Eventually, he agreed to the buccal swab, and we submitted his DNA for comparison. Not surprisingly, he wasn't the killer.

I later googled Janet's name to see if any arrests had been made, only to find out that in 2021, thanks to advancements in DNA technology and dedicated Garden Grove detectives, the case was finally solved. The killer, Terry Dean Hawkins, had died just a year after Janet's murder in 1977 while in the Orange County jail.

This entire series of events highlights how unlikely and intertwined our lives can be. I feel like the theme of my life can be summed up by "What are the odds?"

***

Lately, the world has become obsessed with signs. "No Guns" signs are posted on doors and windows like they're some kind of moral force field, as if a criminal is going to stop, read it, and say, "Well, damn, guess I'll head home."

People ask me all the time, "So… can you even bring your gun in there?" Movie theaters. Malls. Restaurants.

"I'm the police," I tell them. "I take my gun wherever I want." That usually shuts the conversation down, which is fine, because I'm not interested in debating stickers on glass with people who have never stood over a body.

I'm not anti-gun. By the same right, I'm also not a gun fanatic. My gun is a tool. It does a job. It doesn't excite me or bring me joy. It doesn't deserve admiration. I don't collect them or talk about them the way some people talk about watches or cars. I definitely don't want to hear about your concealed carry permit or your gun safe like you're describing a Rolex collection. Shoes, however? Shoes make me happy. Shoes have never ended a life. Except for that one time… but I'll keep going.

I prefer a world where guns belong to the police, the military, and the bad guys. That way, when I see one on the street, I immediately know who I'm dealing with. Somewhere along the line, that clarity disappeared. Now everyone has one, and while I understand wanting a fighting chance, I also understand how often that chance ends with me knocking on someone's door at two in the morning.

What I truly hate are the cutesy guns. Pink ones. Tiffany blue grips. Guns that look like toys. There is nothing adorable about a weapon. Nothing fashionable. If people saw what I see every day—the blood, the panic, the aftermath—I don't think they would want their gun color-coordinated with their purse.

Around that same time, after an abrupt move into a new place, my anxiety crept up in quieter ways. I didn't feel like I had a home, just a space where my things were temporarily parked. I'd seen enough lonely deaths to know how easily people disappear. Quiet apartments. Mail piling up. No one checking in. For a long time, I thought marriage was the fix for that. At least someone would notice if I didn't come home.

Turns out, marriage doesn't guarantee a wellness check either. My ex was a nerd growing up. His mom once paid a coworker to go to prom with him. I thought I'd hit the jackpot. A mama's boy. A bodybuilder. Safe. Someone who knew how to treat women. What I didn't realize was that he was trying to make up for all of the years he'd felt overlooked, and I just happened to be there when he decided to rewrite his story.

So no, I don't trust signs. I trust experience. I trust instincts. I trust the work. I lived two lives at once for six months. One was polished for television; the other was raw and unforgiving, in real alleys with no cameras except maybe the news cameras. The punishment was worth it. The exhaustion was worth it. I got to experience something incredible.

And at the end of the day, when the lights went out and the makeup came off, I was still a homicide detective. Still carrying a gun that was never meant to be cute. Still doing a job no sign on a door could ever make safe.

# CHAPTER 22

## GUNS AND POSES

I have this tight little squad of girlfriends who've basically grown up with me. One of them I've known since kindergarten—the Boss Babe. She came out of the womb with an eye roll, a to-do list, and absolutely no time for nonsense. She's the kind of woman strangers are always telling, "You should smile more," which she finds deeply irritating. The truth is, she's perfectly happy; she just doesn't feel the need to perform joy for anyone else's comfort.

The other two girls joined the crew in high school, back when our biggest problems were deciding between McDonalds and Wendy's for lunch and making sure no one saw us without a gallon of hairspray and red lipstick on.

Somehow, we all ended up taking wildly different career paths. Yolanda is in disaster recovery in IT, which sounds dramatic, but she swears it's mostly fixing things people swear they "didn't touch." Sylvia works in the mortgage industry and can calculate interest rates in her head as long as she has had her morning coffee. And then there's Edith, my kindergarten bestie, the shot caller for a big corporation. She's often featured in *The Wall Street Journal*. But I'll be honest: I love her, but I still have absolutely no idea what her actual job is. Every time I ask, she gives me a different answer that somehow explains nothing. I feel like I'm talking to Tommy from the '90s sitcom *Martin*. She's always "on a call," "heading into a meeting," or "touching base with the team," but no one knows what she actually does. I've just accepted that she's important. Important *adjacent*. Something like that.

We barely see each other because our schedules never match. And when I say "our schedules," I mean *mine*. My girlfriends work civilized hours, which are Monday through Friday, nine to five. They do get to work from home once or twice a week, like normal humans who fold laundry during lunch breaks. Meanwhile, I'm out here thriving in constant chaos and whatever fresh nonsense walks into my day.

Every once in a while, the thought of working from home crosses my mind. Just for a second. Maybe sitting in pajamas, sipping a latte, answering emails without someone screaming in the background. But honestly, there's no career I would rather have than mine… unless I won the lottery and was able to open a pug rescue. Fancy. I think Reba McIntyre wrote a song about me long ago.

I don't usually second guess myself. In my line of work, there's really no time or room for it anyway. The problem with being a homicide detective is you're always aware of how short life is and how death is literally one bad decision away. And these decisions aren't always the ones made by you.

So, maybe we live life more than the average person does or maybe we wallow in sorrow more than the average person does. Who knows... perspective, I guess. I do know that we in Chicago have the highest suicide rate for any police department in the nation. Coincidence? I think not. We also happen to have the highest murder rate in the country. We know death is always lurking around the corner. As for me, I'm always looking for it. When a truck speeds past me, I think all I have to do is turn the steering wheel just a smidge to be the next victim. Our eyes are wide open or wide shut... again, perspective.

We civil servants spend our life talking about what we're gonna do when we retire and then statistically, we retire and then we die within a few years because of the high stress of this job. We're always trying to catch up on sleep, and that never happens. I often say I'll sleep when I'm dead. I just hope that isn't around the corner. As for me, I'm not going to be a statistic. I decided that a long time ago.

The not-so-glamorous details of a woman detective's life: I've been told on more than one occasion that I'm what you can call an acquired taste, or one of those people that you really love, or you really hate. Maybe it's my sunny disposition? I didn't wake up with this resting bitch face, I swear. I like to think I earned it the hard way. I didn't start guarded. I think I used to default to a smile as a kid. But life taught me that softness can often be misread. By the time I became a police officer, my face had learned to hold steady through things that would break most people. The job didn't harden me; my life did. So maybe some people are really meant for this type of job, while others aren't.

You learn pretty quickly that a blank stare gets more respect than a grin. My resting bitch face isn't mean, it's efficient. What people see as an attitude or being stuck up is really my armor from years of staying composed when everything around me was falling apart. I like to call this one of my superpowers. And I actually have more than one.

Beauty is such a strange, subjective thing. People have told me I'm beautiful here and there throughout my life, but I never really grew up *feeling* that way. I was just... me. Dark brown hair that never behaved, pale skin that didn't tan so much as it tried to disappear entirely in the sunlight, and those rosy lips that always looked a little wind-burned no matter the weather. They were too big for my face back then, and kids notice everything, so I wound up with the nickname "Booty Lips" before I even knew what that meant.

I remember being in first grade, sitting cross-legged in front of the TV, watching a show about a ballerina who wanted to have her lips surgically made bigger—"for aesthetic reasons," she said. I didn't even know what "aesthetic" meant, but I knew enough to be confused. Bigger? Why on earth would someone do that on purpose? I was over there trying to hide mine, pressing them together, sucking them in, wishing they would magically shrink overnight. Meanwhile, this girl was asking a doctor to pump hers up like it was some kind of upgrade.

In my little kid brain, it was the most outlandish thing I'd ever heard. You might as well have told me she wanted to make her whole head bigger. I remember just staring at the screen, absolutely baffled, thinking, *Is this really a thing people do?* It was my first introduction to how wildly different we can all see ourselves—and how the world sees us in return.

But I'm confident enough to know that I'm not here to look beautiful. And I'll be the first to admit that it's pretty hard to look good after a thirty-hour shift. My life has kind of been a mix of really feminine jobs and really masculine types of jobs. I joined the army right out of high school. Then I got my first dream job as a flight attendant. I was an aerobics instructor whenever I got bored with my current job... I can't leave out my most interesting job: I was a Hooters Girl. When I joined the police academy, I think some people only knew me as the Hooters Girl.

I could have been an astronaut, but people—both men and women—would still fixate on the fact that I was a waitress at a chicken wing restaurant. The snarky comments went on for years.

After I got to the police department, I found my escape in the most unlikely place—under stage lights in a sequin bikini, putting all of my insecurities out there to be judged by all.

All night, I ran around in a bulletproof vest chasing bad guys and seeing the worst of humanity. During the day, I traded that for endless hours at the gym, the stink of spray tan, and weekly meal prep that often included me carrying a chicken breast in a Ziploc bag in my purse. The same discipline that kept me alive on the streets fueled me on stage. Every day at work was unpredictable. Bodybuilding gave me a weird sense of control that I couldn't find anywhere else. It was pretty simple. Whatever you put in, you got out. Most people think bodybuilding is about vanity, and while that's definitely part of it, for me it was for mental health. Everyone needs an outlet. Some vices are healthier than others.

Every day, I rolled into work with my coolers of food and protein shakes. The guys on my team would make fun of me, but I definitely forced them into healthier eating because we did try to eat lunch as a team, and while I lusted at their occasional cheeseburgers and beef sandwiches, I knew the sacrifice was worth it for me.

# CHAPTER 23

# WHISKEY WITH CONFIDENCE

One Sunday, after a long stretch of late nights and too much coffee and energy drinks, I found myself out at brunch with some of the guys from my team. Marco had picked me up in an Uber since I lived close to him, and by the time we got to the bar, the work brain had finally started to shut off. The place was loud in that daytime drunk kind of way. This meant sunlight pouring through the windows, music a little too upbeat, and people pretending brunch was about food and not mimosas.

We were posted up at a high-top, laughing, decompressing, talking over one another the way cops do when they're finally doing something social. That's when a young guy with blond hair and an easy, unforced confidence walked straight up to our table.

No hesitation. No awkward hovering.

He introduced himself—to me first—and then, without missing a beat, he went down the line shaking hands with every guy I was with. One by one. Calm. Polite. Completely unfazed by the fact that he'd just inserted himself into a group of grown men who spend their lives reading people for a living. I watched my partners clock it instantly. The confidence alone was impressive. Let's be honest, that takes a lot of guts.

Even the guys were impressed. Marco caught my eye and gave me a subtle thumbs-up, like, *Yeah... I don't hate this guy.*

The blond guy smiled, made a quick comment that landed just right, didn't overstay his welcome, and then, quite simply, he asked for my number. No pressure. No performance. Just confidence.

So yeah. He got it. Hello, Mr. Confidence.

Sometimes, even when you're trained to be suspicious of everyone, confidence... real confidence still stands out.

After a few back-and-forth texts, I agreed to go out with Mr. Confidence. Not because I was swept off my feet, but because I'd officially run out of excuses. It was the kind of date you say yes to when your friends start giving you *that* look... the one that says you're dangerously close to adopting another pug and naming your houseplants. I wasn't excited. I was resigned. I told myself it was like ripping off a Band-Aid: quick, uncomfortable, and hopefully over before I had time to talk myself out of it.

Still, I couldn't help being a little excited when I thought about telling my girlfriends. I knew they would assume I would cancel or ghost him at the last minute, so the fact that I was actually going felt like growth. Or at least effort. I hesitated, though, because despite being a literal detective, I didn't know much about Mr. Confidence—and I liked it that way. The second I gave them his name, I knew the mystery would be gone. Within minutes, they would know where he'd grown up, what his parents did for a living, and what kind of pizza he ordered when he was sad. Honestly, at that point, who's the real detective here?

But I was too excited to keep it to myself, so I sent the group text. Predictably, the interrogation began almost immediately.

Edith, always efficient, cut straight to it. "How old is he?" she asked.

"Not that young," I replied.

"Hmmm," she wrote back. "Whatever *that* means."

And just like that, the case was officially open.

I finally got home and collapsed on the couch with the pugs for a few minutes before I peeled myself off the cushions and dragged myself into the shower. I attempted to "get beautified," which for me means putting in just enough effort to look alive and like I maybe sleep more than four hours a night. My partner John kept texting me like he was the one going on this date. He was genuinely more excited than I was, which says a lot. I think he worried about me—either that I was destined to become the neighborhood hermit or that I was secretly a man-hater. I wasn't. I'm not. I'm just picky to a fault and very good at coming up with excuses.

After my marriage imploded, I tried to make sense of it and thought, *How dare he?* I'd been good to my husband. Loyal. Supportive. But hindsight is rude and honest, and now I knew I'd loved the *idea* of our marriage more than I'd actually loved him. By the end, we had nothing in common except an address and a couple routines we were too tired to change. It still didn't stop me from thinking, *Seriously, how dare he?* But anyway. Back to the date.

Mr. Confidence got to choose the location, which already put him ahead of most men who responded with, "I dunno, what do *you* wanna do?" He picked a trendy new speakeasy in Logan Square—cool, dimly lit, cocktails made by some guy with a curled mustache and a vest. One point for Mr. Confidence. He showed up at the exact same time I did. Serendipity? Or just good Uber timing?

I spotted him walking toward me and immediately had the urge to turn and sprint in the other direction. It's my standard pre-date panic: *Abort mission. Save yourself.* But Mr. Confidence was actually more handsome than I remembered. Tall, lean but muscular, shaggy, blond hair—normally not my type, since I usually fell for dark-haired compulsive liars. But maybe blond compulsive liars deserved a chance too. Growth, right?

He ordered whiskey drinks, plural, and downed them pretty quickly. Maybe nerves. Maybe he was just one of those people who drinks like he's trying to dissolve something inside. I sipped my overpriced gin cocktail and tried to look relaxed and not like someone who carries a firearm for a living. We decided to switch locations to a more relaxed neighborhood bar. Nothing fancy, no wine bar vibe, just a place where the lights weren't trying to blind me and the music wasn't mocking my age. He grabbed the tab before I could argue—another point for Mr. Confidence.

We settled into a booth and talked easily. He was from Minnesota, moved to Chicago a few years ago. I silently refused to ask how old he was because then he might ask me, and I wasn't in the mood to tell the truth. I had a suspicion he'd googled me and already knew. Men always pretend they don't, but they do. If I had a dollar for every guy who said, "Oh wow, I didn't even think to look you up," I would be retired in a cabin somewhere with twenty pugs.

The night was… good. Surprisingly good. And that was almost unsettling. Good meant vulnerable, and vulnerable meant risk, and risk meant he could be a killer. I know that sounds dramatic, but my brain is permanently trained to consider that option.

He leaned in closer while we talked, and I caught the mix of fabric softener on his jacket and the Altoid mint he'd just popped. It was strangely comforting. Or alarming. The jury was still out. I mentally made a note of the exits anyway… force of habit.

Eventually, we decided to call it a night and share a taxi home. He sat close, not pushy, and just warm in a way I'd forgotten existed. When the taxi pulled up in front of my building, he told me he wanted to come inside and meet the pugs. *Not tonight, Mr. Confidence.* Not because I was playing games, but because I actually liked the idea of "next time," and that was rare for me. I gave him a soft, friendly goodbye and headed in alone.

For the first time in months, I slept well. Like my brain finally shut up and gave me a break. Maybe Mr. Confidence wasn't a killer after all. Or maybe he was, but at least he was polite and had good hygiene. Win-win?

The next morning, I officially hit my limit on being a responsible adult. Sleep deprivation was catching up with me, and I decided to call off work. I checked the schedule first… everyone was in, so no one would miss me. Perfect. I declared a personal mental health day.

I used a birthday gift card to book a massage. The place isn't fancy, but it's close, and I found rock-star parking right out front. I was twenty minutes early, which was dangerous for me because sitting in my car always invited strangers to approach me and ask things I didn't want to answer.

Inside, I shoved my bag, shoes, and gun into a tiny locker, threw on a robe, and grabbed the cucumber water they acted like came from the Fountain of Youth. I sat in the relaxation room, trying to zone out, when a middle-aged woman with frizzy brown hair plopped down across from me. No makeup, robe too big, looked like she'd just come from a Groupon meditation class.

I gave her a polite half-smile, the kind that says, *Please don't talk to me,* which of course meant she immediately started talking to me. It was her birthday. Her boyfriend surprised her with a massage and a trip to Boston for a Patriots game. I told her that sounded amazing. It didn't. It sounded like something I would fake an injury to avoid. She went on about football players I'd never heard of and never would. I told her she was lucky. She agreed enthusiastically.

Then she told me she was a bartender at some late-night cop bar I'd never been to. I internally debated whether to say I was a detective, because the second I did, she would ask if I knew Officer So-and-So. I always have to answer with the same line: "There are twelve thousand of us." People act like we're all roommates. She finally asked what I do, and because lying takes too much effort today, I told her. She lit up and said she had "experience with cops." I assumed she meant from the bar.

"No, actually. I served time."

Of course she did.

She said she wouldn't tell me why she went to prison. Spoiler: that always means they want to tell you exactly why. I refused to ask. She broke within three seconds. Just as she was about to confess her sins, my massage therapist—a stocky Russian woman built like she used to deadlift small trees—stepped out and called, "Michele."

Saved by the Siberian bell.

The massage was amazing. She found every knot I'd collected from years of heavy vests and sleeping like a feral raccoon. I almost fell asleep. When it was over, I stalled in the locker room long enough to avoid the convict. *Not today, Martha Stewart. Not today.*

By the time I got home, I felt lighter. Not fixed, not magical—just lighter. And because I was feeling bold, I texted Mr. Confidence back when he checked in to see how I was doing. "I'm sorry about the other night," he said. "I was pretty wasted."

"No worries," I assured him.

We chatted. It felt easy. For once, my life didn't feel like it was spiraling or exploding.

Maybe… just maybe I needed a night like that. Or a person like that. Or just a reminder that I wasn't broken or doomed or destined to live in a trench coat, yelling, "I got another murder!" forever. Maybe this was my reset button.

My phone went off at that point and I saw it was another text from Mr. Confidence. He wanted to know when my next day off is. Most guys don't understand the whole schedule I have. I almost never have weekends off and even on my days off, I often end up working or spending my day on the phone with other cops, trying to give information on cases or bosses inquiring about cases or informants calling. I always feel like there's never enough hours in the day to get everything done. Just when you catch up with a case, you get called to do an interview or boom, someone else dies.

I told Mr. Confidence that I would be off in a few days and promised to save some time to see him.

He basically worked a nine to five, with weekends off. This could never go anywhere, but it could be fun. Maybe I should give him one more shot. He didn't ask me many questions about my job, which struck me as kind of odd. It's not like every day you meet a female homicide detective, right?

Mr. Confidence said he was going to sleep. It was 9:00 p.m. I was slightly put off by that. I didn't think people actually went to sleep that early.

"This is definitely a bad idea," I reminded myself.

# CHAPTER 24

## FELONITUS

I walked into work and was immediately bombarded by detectives on the robbery team who asked me to search their female prisoner. There was a female police officer who worked the desk downstairs and could easily have done this search before I arrived, but I'm sure they were just afraid to ask because she was kind of crabby. The officer was an older female who would be cute except for the fact that the scowl she'd been wearing for the past hundred years had etched a permanent frown into her face. She was the kind of person who questions why another younger female officer is working the desk and answering the phones while she's forced to work harder than everyone. In other words, she was far more worried about other people than she was with herself. Some people aren't meant to run and gun after the bad guys. They're better off doing reports and things that I myself have zero desire to do. It takes all kinds in this diverse department. Blondie was just mean. She wasn't nice to the men unless they showed her special attention and she was just plain awful to other female officers. She also hated me today. Go figure.

"So, where's your prisoner?" I asked the robbery detectives.

They escorted me to Interview Room A.

This woman was wearing a bad pink wig and was apparently in custody for running some kind of financial crime scam where she was stealing from senior citizens. I immediately hated her for that but figured I would do them a favor. There was only a small percentage of women who worked in the Detective Division with me. As a whole, the police department was still predominantly male, but in the Detective Division, in the Violent Crimes Section, I was usually the only female there at night aside from Blonde Betty, who was a police officer, not a detective. She only answered the phone and certainly didn't do female searches. The perks of that were that I didn't have to share the bathrooms with any other detectives. The cons were that I was stuck searching every single female prisoner who walked into the building, and I was forced to play babysitter, mom, or confidante to every female witness or victim.

Doing a custodial search of anyone isn't fun but in general, women seem to have more hiding spots, and those hiding spots often don't smell good. I think I've found every kind of contraband known to man while searching women. You name it and I've probably seen it: drugs, guns, knives, money, and even food. I guess you never know when hunger might strike.

Speaking of food, I recently came up with an anecdote regarding carrying food in your purse. Don't do it. I can't tell you how many times I've looked through a deceased person's purse and found an old grilled cheese sandwich or a piece of chicken. I'm, like, c'mon. That's a good way to get sick, though by the time I find it, getting sick is no longer a concern for them. So, another rule that I can add to my rule book is No More Carrying Food in My Purse Ever. No matter what the circumstance is.

My partner John will remind me if I even get that look in my eye of, "It's just a sandwich. It will stay." He quickly reminds me of the girl who took her friend's prescription anxiety medicine in order to relax while she got her first bikini wax. She decided to couple that medicine with some wine, and... Well, she died. It was an awfully sad situation, but it always reminds me to tell people to never, ever share their meds with someone because it could result in you being charged with murder if they happen to have an adverse reaction like this girl did. In an attempt to identify this girl, I looked through her purse, where I found a nasty old grilled cheese. So, it's apparent that this girl didn't make the best decisions in general. Her friend then freely admitted that she'd given her friend Xanax to calm her down while she waxed her. She claimed to be an aesthetician. But she didn't have a license and operated out of her house. I found the murderous wax pot, which was filled with little hairs that were probably pubic hairs. Gross. She was operating a waxing business out of her tiny apartment in the River North Area. She had no mal intentions and the case went nowhere, but I always believed she should have been charged with something.

So, since then, I've vowed to never carry food with me anymore. Another problem with being the only "broad," as I've been called, is I'm also supposed to be the supplier of women's hygiene products. It still surprises me when men become so uncomfortable when a woman talks about her period. Don't most men have moms, wives, daughters who get their period? A man shouldn't shut down when he hears the word "period." I always have male officers come up to me and say, "Can you help her? She has her period," as if it's a terminal illness. So, I keep a stash of pads and tampons for the occasional accident some female arrestee might have. I should claim this stuff on my taxes.

Today, I was asked to search the pink-haired girl who loved to rob grandmas. When I walked into the room, she was frantic. She was literally in tears, and not the fake tears I was used to seeing. She was in a full panic. Part of me wanted to say, "This is what you deserve for stealing from Grandma," but the other part of me felt bad for anyone who has anxiety. Because I'm claustrophobic, the thought of being trapped inside a room with no windows freaks the hell out of me. Thank God I'm on the good side of the law because as a criminal, I could never survive being trapped anywhere.

Pink Hair told me that she has horrible anxiety and started begging me not to leave. I decided to chat with her for a minute and learned that her boyfriend had set up this elaborate scheme and she kind of just went along with it.

"Well," I told her, "I can't help you with this case because another detective is handling it."

She then asked me to stay with her for a little while, hold her hand, and "count" with her.

"Count?" I asked.

Yes. She explained that it's a coping mechanism she learned from therapy. When she's having a panic attack she counts, and it helps calm her down. Maybe she would have less anxiety if she decided to abort the life of crime and get a job. Just a thought.

*Hmm*, I thought to myself, *maybe I should count.* Wine actually worked well for me, but maybe I would try this next time. So, even though I was much too busy to be sitting there counting, I decided to stay for a few minutes and put some funds in my karma bank. Hopefully, this would change my luck.

So, against everything in me that said don't touch her hand, I obliged. She was standing in front of a metal toilet with no toilet seat, and the sink next to it wasn't equipped with soap. We stood there while she counted and cried. Her trembling hands were sweaty and cold. Her chipped, dirty fake nails were touching the palm of my hand.

I finally dropped her clammy hands, told her I would be back to check on her, and got out of the room. But first, she needed to hand over her wig to me. *Sorry, honey. That thing can't go to lock-up with you, but you'll get it back later.*

About four hours later, she found out she was being charged with a few felonies. She literally collapsed, and the detectives immediately called for an ambulance to take her to the hospital. The firemen arrived upstairs with all of their toys. I pretended to be looking for something so I could get a quick look. Not too bad, but none of these guys were from the firemen's calendar. I needed to stay away from firemen and all city workers anyway. When would I learn?

Anytime anyone in our custody says they aren't feeling well, we have to call an ambulance. It's usually a ploy done by offenders who somehow think if they go to the hospital, they won't go to jail. It's called "felonitus," the fatal illness that occurs right before you're charged with a felony or when you have a nice bag of drugs shoved up your butt.

However, shortening their stay in jail? That's never the case. If anything, it could prolong their stay. If they miss the bus that transports them to court to see the judge, so be it. This is Cook County, where the bond is low and the killers run amok. A low bond or no bond is imminent.

# CHAPTER 25

## LINEUP SHEETS

I got into my car and tried to organize my notes from the crime scene and put my reports in chronological order so I could use it to type the progress reports later on, after I fueled up with coffee and a late night breakfast. As I was sitting in the car, I saw a female police officer seated at the light. She was parked and obviously had just cleared from a traffic stop. She was young and appeared agitated, and her face was void of any real emotion. It reminded me of when I was a new police officer in the 14th District, trying to make a name for myself.

My friend Joel, who was also assigned to the 14th District, called me with some bad news. Someone had scratched my name off the line-up sheets and scrawled "Bitch" over my last name, Wood. The lineup sheets were posted every evening and had the assignments for the next day. The sheets showed you which beat you would be working, what your special attention was (if any) and, most importantly, who you would be working with. Some people were lucky enough to be assigned to a regular partner, whom they worked with most of the time. But even regular partners got changed up once in a while for a myriad of reasons. For instance, if a certain district assignment or detail required at least one female, a set of female partners could be split up for the night and be forced to work with someone else. Some officers didn't have regular partners and kind of just floated around or worked 99, which meant they worked solo.

The lineup sheets were our roll call, last names, partners, beat numbers, and squad cars. New officers always drew the lemons: squad cars without air conditioning, broken radios, or a PDT (police data terminal) that barely functioned.

A PDT was our version of high-tech at the time, though by today's standards it was laughable. It gave us our assignments and let us send messages to the dispatcher or other officers. Picture AOL chatrooms on a tiny green screen. If you're old enough, you're already hearing that dial-up shriek followed by, "You've got mail." That was about the extent of it, long before the internet took over our lives.

Without a working PDT, you had to actually pay attention when the dispatcher called you. My normal beat call back then was 1444. I would answer back, "1444," and then scribble notes as fast as possible—location, suspect description, and what weapon we were supposedly up against. Half the time, you would be flying down the street with lights and sirens before realizing you couldn't remember a single word she'd said. So yes, even a clunky PDT was worth its weight in gold. But back to the insult.

*Really? Bitch?* I thought to myself. *That was the best they could come up with?* On my beat car, we had Officers Little, Johnson, and Wood, which meant that on any given night, you could find Little/Wood, Little/Johnson, or Johnson/Wood listed on the sheet. There was plenty of material there if someone wanted to get creative.

When I got to work, I checked the sheet myself to verify what Joel had said. Joel clearly needed glasses. It didn't say "Bitch." It said "Dike."

I actually laughed. Thank God. I would take "Dike" over "Bitch" any day. "Bitch" probably meant I'd turned you down. "Dike" meant you were upset because you knew you never had a chance.

That's the kind of petty nonsense that floated around the department. It's also the kind of thing people never think about when they ask me what it's like to be a homicide detective. They imagine every day is non-stop action—crime scenes, interrogations, courtroom drama.

The truth is, most days are paperwork, court appearances, and meetings. But in between the mundane, there are days when you're chasing down murderers, pulling off undercover stings, or making split-second calls that could make—or end—careers. Those are the days that stick with you.

# CHAPTER 26

## RUNNING ON EMPTY

I was home and couldn't sleep. Again. Nothing new there. I've had insomnia since I was a kid, but years of stepping over dead bodies and listening to raw, animal screams from families forced to stand behind crime scene tape while their loved one is being poked, prodded, flipped over, and photographed? Yeah. That'll do a number on whatever was left of anyone's sleep.

And since I'm not allowed to take edibles or smoke weed, I go with the second-best option: red wine. I've never been much of a drinker, but one little glass can take the edge off even the worst day. I am, as most would call it, a lightweight.

So, I pulled out a twenty-dollar California red from Sonoma Valley, half of which would inevitably go to waste… and queued up Amy Winehouse while I sat there thinking about all of my questionable life decisions.

I managed six hours of actual sleep before I was up again, extra early, because today I had court. We were supposed to start trial for a murder that had happened years ago. So much for the whole "speedy trial" thing. And if this actually went to trial, it was about to throw a giant wrench into my big plans.

Most people don't understand how *slowly* the wheels of justice turn in Chicago. While I might be working three brand-new murder cases in one week, I can still get called in to court to testify on a homicide I caught years ago. Two years. Three. Sometimes six. The past never really lets go. If you want to survive in this job, multitasking isn't just a skill. It's muscle memory. You live in the present while being constantly dragged into your own history.

But I'd felt it lately, like I was steps away from a breakthrough. Usually, once you finally get a trial date, it gets pushed back at least three times. Everyone is overworked: State's Attorneys, public defenders, all of them—and me, of course. I have friends on both sides. Honestly, I think public defenders secretly hate their jobs but can't admit it because they went in all noble, thinking, "I'm going to help people," and then reality hits and… people suck.

I got to the courthouse and punched in at 9:08 a.m. Of course, we get a seven-minute cushion, and of course, I missed it by one minute. Story of my life. So now, I was losing fifteen minutes of pay over sixty seconds. Fabulous.

The Criminal Court building is the cesspool of the city. You can literally ride the elevator with the person you arrested—or worse, their entire family. Makes for a cozy trip.

While I was at court on a couple older murder cases getting ready to go trial, I met up with the State's Attorney on Tina Gerber's sexual assault case, who told me they were "thinking" of offering our neighborhood rapist Tyrone a deal. *A deal? Are you kidding me?* This case was locked. Why on earth would we hand this guy another chance to ruin someone's life?

I said nothing out loud, but my inner voice was practically flipping tables. I was wise enough to know that "thinking" about offering him a deal meant they'd already offered him a deal. And I was right. I set this aside and headed over to check in on my other cases.

I checked in and met with my favorite State's Attorney, Maria Augustus, on a murder case. I knew we were going to hit at least ten tangents before we even attempted to touch the case file. She would rant about men, then launch into stories about Mykonos, where she has a house and fully plans to retire once she's done terrorizing the legal system.

Today, she was going off about a guy she'd been dating in Greece and how she'd decided—last week—to marry him. On a whim. I said congrats, but she looked like she was waiting for someone to validate her life choices. Without doubt, there were shots of Ouzo involved.

Then she pivoted again, this time to how she finally adopted a healthy lifestyle and got her hormones in check long enough to start to try having a baby. I couldn't even lie; I was interested. Intrigued, actually.

Anyway, after the saga of her new husband, her Mykonos house, and the girls who rented her Michigan vacation home and managed to flood the toilet, she finally delivered actual case news. She spit it out in the first five minutes… classic Maria. The case was continued. She would call me with a new date.

Success. I could hit the gym and still get ready for work as soon as Maria finished the rest of her story. I jumped in the car, but it took fifteen minutes to get out of the parking lot because all of the employees and jurors were trying to beat the rush hour traffic. We call this the mass exodus. But of course, I got onto the highway and traffic was a bitch as usual. I decided to stay on the highway even though it was backed up instead of driving through the hood. This way, I could turn off my Spidey senses and try to unwind and listen to music. This helps me slowly get out of cop mode and decompress. Otherwise, I have to worry about being car jacked or offered drugs on every corner.

Driving home from court using the streets would mean I had to drive through the Lawndale and Garfield Park neighborhoods in Chicago. This area of the city was the scene of the Chicago Riots more than fifty years ago. Driving down Madison Avenue basically transports you back in time, because literally nothing has changed and it looks almost exactly as it did after the 1968 riots and subsequent fires and looting. The old mayor back then allegedly said he would never rebuild the area, and it seems as though he kept his word. This has given way to the poverty in the area which, of course, leads to desperation, which leads to open air drugs markets and, shocker... crime, namely murder.

# CHAPTER 27

# A DIFFERENT KIND OF BEAT

In the midst of the craziness with my case load and my personal life, I was promoted to sergeant. I'd taken the first part of the promotional exam a few years earlier. I didn't really prepare for the exam because I didn't really want to be a supervisor. I was lucky enough to score fairly well and was on the list for promotion. The promotion had come up at the absolute wrong time for me, so I decided to defer it and re-visit the idea when it came up again. People thought I was crazy, but I knew I needed to finish up some of my cases before I could even think about moving on. Getting promoted meant that I would be going back to patrolling the streets in a marked squad car. It almost felt like a demotion to me.

I finally decided to take the promotion to sergeant when it was offered to me again about a year later. That was the hardest transition I ever had on this job. I went from working high-profile murder cases to approving traffic crash reports and patrolling the streets of the 19th District on the midnight shift. Midnights was brutal. I thought that because of all of the overtime I'd worked as a detective, midnights would be a piece of cake. They weren't. The 19th District was considered a good assignment, one of the better ones, actually. When I got the call that I was headed there as a brand-new sergeant, I knew I'd lucked out. The area was nothing like the districts where you age ten years in one shift. The neighborhoods were cleaner, the calls were a little calmer, and people actually walked their dogs at night like they trusted the universe.

The district covered a big mix of communities including Lakeview, Uptown, Lincoln Park and, of course, Boystown, which brought its own energy. Rainbow flags everywhere, bars packed seven nights a week, drag shows that could put Broadway to shame. It was diverse, loud, colorful, and never boring. You could go from taking a report about a stolen bicycle to mediating an argument between two neighbors who'd known each other since the '80s. On a good day, it felt quirky, funny, and full of characters.

But here's the thing: being in a good district doesn't mean the job itself magically gets easier. I was still a new sergeant, which meant I was learning everything the long way, making mistakes, second-guessing myself, and pretending I knew what I was doing. Everyone around me had their rhythm, their contacts, and their shortcuts. I'd been in the Detective Division so long that when I got promoted to sergeant, I realized I didn't even remember how to fill out a traffic ticket. And there I was, trying to earn my place without looking like I was trying too hard.

So yes, 19 was a good district, and I was genuinely happy to be there. It was the kind of place other sergeants wished they could land. But being in a good neighborhood doesn't change the weight of the work. Crime is still crime. Trauma is still trauma.

My sleeping problems were on a whole new level as I was now forced to sleep during the day. And that was only when I didn't have to go to court to testify on old cases. I spent about six months in misery before I started getting used to it. I finally impressed enough bosses and was offered a position supervising a tactical team. A tactical team is basically a plain-clothed unit that doesn't respond to calls but instead supports the beat officers by focusing on gang violence, suppression, and apprehending offenders. My tactical team of ten burly men and one tough-as-nails woman had to teach me the basics again. In return, I taught them how to build cases. Investigations, big or small… that's my wheelhouse.

Our mission on the 19th District Tactical Team was straightforward: hit the robberies and gang violence head-on. Some days, that meant digging into data and conducting surveillance. Other days, it meant sprinting after offenders before they could disappear into the city.

And then there were the bizarre days, like my last week on the team, when we went undercover to catch guys selling fake Elton John concert tickets on Craigslist. It was chaos from start to finish: wrong location, no money, a surprise accomplice, and backup from one of my officers who thought when I mentioned "Subway" I meant the train station, not the sandwich shop. But somehow, we pulled it off. We cuffed them, avoided a brawl, and I learned not to trust officers who don't speak fluent Chicago.

That was nothing compared to the week that followed.

One late night, I found myself calling off a fifty-one-minute not-quite-a-chase down Lake Shore Drive that spiraled into a SWAT hostage situation in Englewood. By the end of that twenty-four-hour shift, I was exhausted, wired, and according to the gossip mill, a legend-in-the-making. "Who the hell is that female sergeant? She's got balls."

The truth is, I was terrified. My heart pounded so hard I could hear it in my ears. Was I making the right call? Should I have terminated sooner? Was I putting officers' careers—and lives—on the line? The fear never really goes away. You just learn to carry it.

Yes, it was eventually a chase. Three minutes and twenty seconds of the fifty-something minutes constituted a chase, and I was okay with that. But when the dust settled, the offenders were in custody, the victims were safe, and justice had the final word.

We pursued those guys because they'd broken the law and hurt innocent people, and I wasn't going to let them get away.

That day... the good guys won.

Aside from that craziness, I was also getting ready for a few high-profile murder trials on the horizon.

I was the lead detective on two of these cases, so I could expect to be on the stand for several hours testifying. So, I had lots of studying to do. In the following weeks, I actually had three murder trials. Lots went into each but thankfully, in each case, the killers were found guilty.

Aside from arresting bad guys, I also put five people in prison for essentially the rest of their lives... all in a couple weeks' work.

***

In 2018, things finally started to calm down, and I was in a good place. I'd settled into being a tactical team sergeant. The job made sense. I wasn't constantly waiting for the next shoe to drop. Life felt steady in a way that almost made me suspicious, because that's usually when something happens. And then something did—but in the best possible way.

Out of nowhere, I got this offer to do a web-based after-show for the Bravo hit *Imposters*. The show was called *True Cons*, and I was supposed to co-host it with a prominent television personality named Georgia Hardstark. I already knew who she was before anyone even finished pitching it to me. I'd watched her way back on *Tripping Out with Allie & Georgia*, and by then she was already huge from *My Favorite Murder*. I was a fan, not in a weird way, just in a "this person is smart and funny and asks the right questions" way. So, when I heard her name attached, I didn't hesitate. I was in.

They flew me out to California, and there wasn't much time to overthink it, which was probably a good thing. I landed, got my bearings, and basically went straight to the set. Georgia and I met and immediately got to work. No awkward small talk. No trying to feel each other out. We just clicked. The chemistry was instant and completely unforced, which is rare and kind of impossible to fake. You either have it or you don't, and we did. The whole thing ended up being, hands down, the most fun I've ever had doing television.

I was her co-host, but I was also there as the interrogation expert. The idea behind *True Cons* was that we would walk through the storyline of *Imposters*, which was a scripted, dramatic world of con artists… and then stop and say, "Okay, but here's how this actually works in real life." We would break down the psychology, the tells (changes in behavior that reveal what someone is thinking), the lies people tell, and the ones they don't even realize they're telling. We weren't just recapping the show; we were dissecting it.

And then we would bring in people who had really lived that life. Former CIA agents. Masters of disguise. People whose entire careers were built on deception and identity. The conversations were smart and fast and genuinely interesting. It was just honest. Georgia was curious in a way that made the whole thing feel natural, like two people sitting there going, "Wait—*that* part is real?"

We filmed six episodes in one day. Six. Full. Episodes. Six wardrobe changes. Constantly moving, constantly resetting. And somehow, none of it felt exhausting. It definitely didn't feel like work. There was a lot of laughing, a lot of "wait, what?" moments, and a lot of realizing how weird it was that my job—this thing rooted in violence and interrogation and human darkness—was now translating into something people could watch on their phones after a TV show.

*True Cons* aired on Bravo's website and app after each episode of *Imposters*. It lived in that space between entertainment and reality, between fiction and the kind of stuff I'd spent years seeing up close. And for me, it landed at exactly the right moment. I wasn't trying to prove myself. I was just doing something that felt fun and natural and surprisingly easy.

It's strange how life works like that. You grind for years. And then, right when things settle, you end up on a soundstage in California, talking about con artists with someone you already respect, realizing that sometimes the calm doesn't mean the story is over. Sometimes it's just setting the stage for something you never saw coming.

In between all of this, I also snuck away for a four-day trip to Paris. Most people would think less than four days in Paris is a waste, but I've learned to savor every moment of every day, so four days was just enough. I traveled with my girlfriends Sylvia, Yolanda, and Edith. We're all pretty easy travelers. We like the same things, for the most part. So, we're almost exactly the same but also have nothing in common, if that makes any sense. Outside of work, I spend considerable time with people who aren't the police.

We have interesting conversations, but most of it doesn't involve crimes. I know they respect my job, but they could never understand some of the things I see on a daily basis.

Imagine that! They truly listen and don't judge.

Although I loved working in the 19th District on the tactical team, I started to feel that old familiar itch again, the one that never really goes away. Once you've been a detective, there's something about it that stays in your blood. The chase. The puzzles. The nights that don't end until you get the answer you're looking for. I missed it. Badly.

But here's the thing about leaving the Detective Division: once you're out, you're out. It's like trying to crawl back into a locked room after you've already handed in the key. People don't get second chances there. Maybe they're gonna call the lucky ones here. But too often, that call almost never comes.

Then, one afternoon, my phone rang. It was my old commander. The second I saw his name flash on the screen, I knew it meant something big. He didn't waste any time—asked if I would be willing to come back to the Detective Division, to take over as the Sex Crimes Sergeant and the DNA Sergeant. The guy who currently had both roles was stepping away, and they needed someone who could handle the chaos that came with that territory.

Before he even finished the sentence, I said yes. Hell yes. I was elated… the kind of elation that makes your heart race and your palms sweat because you know life just opened a door that's usually nailed shut.

A few days later, I spoke with the outgoing sergeant, Jimmy Lamperis. He practically sighed with relief when I told him I was coming in to replace him. He'd been running Sex Crimes solo for too long and was burned out. Every Wednesday, he had to sit through meetings with rape advocates and community organizations, who were mostly women. Some of them, understandably, weren't thrilled about a man leading those conversations. Jimmy wasn't exactly the "warm and fuzzy" type either. He joked that I was saving his life by taking it off his hands, and maybe I was. His joke was always, "I'm terrible at sex. Ask my wife." That joke was used over and over again at meetings and usually ran flat.

It's funny, because I'd spent most of my career in places where being a woman in law enforcement meant I was the odd one out. People weren't used to seeing women in tactical gear or running a scene. But in Sex Crimes, it was the reverse. Here, they didn't want men around. Suddenly, my gender was an advantage. The irony wasn't lost on me.

Still, leaving my tactical team wasn't easy. Those guys were like family. We'd been through some wild cases together. We'd had long nights, adrenaline-fueled chases, and the kind of arrests that make you feel like all of the heartache is worth it. Most tactical teams get their activity by chasing radio calls, responding to whatever comes in. But I didn't run my team like that. I ran them like detectives. I taught them to think, to dig, and to connect dots instead of just chasing numbers.

And they loved it. You could see it in the way they started carrying themselves… with a little more pride, a little more edge. They weren't just arresting people anymore; they were solving things.

One memorable night, a young woman walked into the 19th District front desk, upset and embarrassed. Someone had scammed her with fake concert tickets. Most people would have brushed it off as a civil matter, not worth the time. But not me. I took that case. We dug in, tracked down the scammer, and built it out like any other investigation. It might not have been a homicide but it was a mystery, and that's what I lived for.

So when I transitioned into the Sex Crimes position as a Sergeant of Detectives, I was genuinely excited. I've always been fascinated by DNA, the science, the patterns, the way a microscopic trace could crack open an entire case. As the DNA Sergeant, part of my job was handling CODIS hits—the Combined DNA Index System. Every time we got a CODIS hit, it meant there was a story waiting to be told. Someone thought they'd gotten away with something, but science had other plans.

I got to work on some incredible cases. Cases that never see the light of day in the news, but that quietly deliver justice years after everyone has forgotten. I worked closely with detectives I'd known for years and, over time, I started building my own little crew. We weren't an official team, but that's what we became—a team built on trust, instinct, and grit.

My old partner used to call us "the sexy detectives." It started as a joke, but it stuck. Maybe it was the name, maybe it was the attitude, but we owned it. We were solving sex crimes, running DNA hits, connecting dots across cold cases, and we did it with precision, persistence, and just enough edge to keep people guessing.

There was something raw about that work. It got under your skin. Every file you opened carried a piece of someone's trauma. But it also carried their chance at closure—and if you've ever worked those cases, you know that's what keeps you coming back. You might lose sleep, but you gain something far more important: purpose.

# CHAPTER 28

# NOTHING WRONG WITH
# A HAPPY ENDING

Remember the restructuring in 2012? At the time, it was sold as progress. Fewer areas. More efficiency. A smarter way to police the city. By 2020, it was clear that experiment hadn't worked.

Response times were slower. Accountability was diluted. The distance between detectives and the neighborhoods they were responsible for had grown too wide. So the department did what large institutions often do. The CPD admitted, quietly, that the idea might have been a mistake and decided to restructure again. This time, the plan was to go back to what had worked before. Area Four and Area Five would reopen. We would return to five detective areas instead of three.

On paper, it was just a logistical shift. In reality, it was massive. Area Four, in particular, was about to become one of the most dangerous assignments in the city. It meant starting from scratch—new units, new supervisors, detectives pulled from all over to staff it. The kind of place that would demand experience, instincts, and people willing to absorb the worst of humanity without blinking. I was ready for a change but wasn't sure if this was the change I wanted. I only lived a few blocks away from Area Three. Was I crazy?

I mean… I loved working sex crimes. The work mattered, and I was good at it. But the pull of homicide never really leaves you once it gets into your system. That familiar gravity took over, and when one of the most respected lieutenants and a commander—leaders people would give anything to work for—offered me a spot on a homicide team in Area Four, I didn't hesitate. Area Four sat at Harrison and Kedzie, tucked upstairs from the old 11th District, which is the same ground where modern police work was invented. That's not hyperbole. The systems, the structure, the idea of what investigative policing even *was*, all came from there.

But if police work was invented downstairs, it was perfected upstairs. That's what people said anyway. And people believed it.

Area Four carried an allure that was hard to explain to anyone who hadn't worked there. It wasn't about the building; it was about what it represented. The detectives assigned there had bragging rights, whether they admitted it out loud or not. Saying you worked Area Four meant something. It still does. It was silly in some ways, pure cop mythology in others, but mythology matters in this job. It shapes how people see themselves and how hard they're willing to push.

The detectives were considered the *real* police, the ones who handled the worst neighborhoods, the ugliest crimes, the cases that didn't make sense and didn't wrap up neatly. Area Four wasn't for the lighthearted. It demanded instincts, tough skin, and the kind of confidence that only comes from being wrong enough times to finally get it right.

You didn't go to Area Four to be comfortable. You went there to be tested. And if you survived it and if you proved you belonged, you carried that badge of honor with you long after you left.

That was the pull. That was the legend. I accepted.

There was just one small problem.

I was six months pregnant… and hiding it… quite well, if you ask me.

So, at this point, my life looked slightly different than it had just a few years before. A couple years after I'd left the Detective Division, Marco Garcia and I began dating… each other. When we were on the same team, we were both married to other people, but we'd always been good friends who had each other's back.

That said, I'm not going to pretend I was blind. I knew he was good-looking. I noticed it the same way you notice things in passing and then move on. There was some light, harmless flirting, the kind that lives safely on the surface and never goes anywhere. Nothing salacious. Just two people with history, shared humor, and good chemistry working long hours in close quarters.

Our connection didn't start at work anyway. We'd gone to high school together. Or more accurately, HE went to high school with me. He claims he noticed me back then, even if I don't remember noticing him. Life pulled us in different directions and years later, we landed on the same homicide team, older, married, and living completely separate lives.

Much later… after the team, long after those marriages ended, we found ourselves unexpectedly single in freakishly similar circumstances. We dated other people. We lived our lives. But the familiarity was still there, the ease, the history.

Eventually, we stopped pretending it was coincidence. Not because of something that happened back then, but because of everything that didn't. At some point, we decided to stop fighting the idea altogether and see if there was a real possibility of being with each other.

We'd each had our fair share of relationships—some messy, some meaningful—but somehow, we circled back to each other. It wasn't until much later that we found ourselves together when the timing was finally right.

Looking back, I can see how it all makes sense now. People had always said how good we looked together. It was one of those things people would throw out in passing, like a comment you hear but don't take seriously. I never really imagined it before, couldn't picture it in any real way. After all, we were always working side by side, partners in crime in a different sense, a team. I was his wing woman, his confidante, the one who had his back no matter what. I was also his annoying female friend who caused many of his former girlfriends angst. There were times I thought we were like oil and water; he was the steady one, the calm in the storm, and I was the one with the questions, the curiosity, the energy. But then something shifted. It wasn't sudden. It wasn't like some grand moment where everything clicked into place. It was more subtle, gradual… a realization, I guess, that one day, after so many years of working together, of getting each other through the worst of days and celebrating the smallest victories, that maybe there was no one better to be with than your best friend.

And that's what Marco became to me: my best friend. My partner, not at work, but in life. Every time I reached for something, he was there, always close by. Every time I needed to vent or laugh or just talk through the crazy thoughts in my head, he was the one I turned to.

There were multiple times when my car ran out of gas or I locked my keys in my apartment. It wasn't because I was overwhelmed by cases or falling apart; it was because I was constantly multitasking, usually doing three things at once and not especially well. I was answering calls while getting dressed, making mental lists while walking out the door, half present in whatever task was right in front of me. I would ignore the gas light because I was already thinking about the next errand, the next obligation, the next thing I needed to knock out. I would close my apartment door on autopilot, already moving on to the next task, only to realize I'd left the keys behind. It was less chaos and more inefficiency. I call it death by distraction… small, avoidable mistakes that came from trying to do too much at the same time.

And in those quiet moments, after everything settled down, I realized there was nothing about Marco I didn't know. There was no part of him that felt like a stranger. I'd seen him at his best, at his worst, in the moments that made him proud and the ones that made him question everything. There was no pretending, no awkwardness. Just *us*.

And somewhere, in the middle of all that familiarity, I saw it. I saw him not just as a partner, not just as the guy who sat next to me during late-night report writing or the one who had to clean up after my messes that occurred from my lack of patience or my personal breakdowns. I saw him as someone I could actually be with, really be with. No pretense. No pressure. Just two people who had already shared everything, who had seen each other through the worst and had come out on the other side with a trust deeper than anything I'd ever known.

For all of the people who said we would look good together, it finally hit me: they were right. But it wasn't about how we looked on the outside. It was about how we fit together on the inside, how our lives had already been intertwined for so long that it was impossible to untangle them. All of those years working together, laughing and arguing, keeping each other sane in a job that made you question everything… it was all leading up to this moment.

Together, we built something real. And that, to me, was the most beautiful thing of all. A quiet house, my daughter, my husband now, my real Prince Charming, the one who showed up after my whole world imploded… this was the life I wasn't sure I would ever get. The one I didn't think I deserved. It wasn't something I ever expected, but in hindsight, it feels like the most natural thing in the world. It's funny how life works out that way. From being his wing woman to being his equal, to now sharing a name, his name, and maybe even his nickname… Mrs. 312.

And honestly? It feels right. Like we've been writing this story together all along, even when we didn't know the ending.

What I didn't know then… standing in that quiet, finally steady place, was that I wasn't at the end of anything at all. I thought the wild chapters were behind me. The chaos, the long nights, the weight of other people's tragedies carried home in the seams of my jacket… I believed those doors had closed. I thought I'd earned the calm, that the story had gently settled into its final shape. But life has a way of smiling politely while it sharpens the plot. Because just when I thought my adventures were over, just when I believed I'd stepped out of the storm for good, I was being called back in. This time, it wasn't as the young detective trying to prove herself, but as a leader. Back to homicide. Back to the place that had forged me. Back with a different badge of responsibility, a different kind of fear, and a whole new level of madness waiting patiently around the corner.

The cases would be darker, the stakes higher, the decisions heavier—and I would no longer be answering to someone else's voice, but to my own. So, if this story sounds like an ending, it is—but only in the way the last deep breath works before you run headfirst into what comes next. Because the truth is, the calm didn't mean the craziness was gone. It just meant I was finally ready for it. And if I've learned anything at all, it's that the moment you think you know what's coming next… you're usually wrong.

What I didn't realize was that I'd only stepped out long enough to be ready to walk back in. Homicide was waiting, and this time I wouldn't be learning how to survive it. I would be leading others through it.

# REFLECTION

What these cases taught me... and what I want the reader to walk away with... is how darkness can come from places you least expect. A mother's love, a son's entitlement. Trust and betrayal. I stepped into some of my most memorable investigations thinking, *Another homicide*. But I left thinking about legacy, choices, and the line between protector and destroyer.

As a homicide detective sergeant, I walk the line between tragedy and justice every day. Yet these cases will always stay with me because of what they ask us to do... to see through the bullshit, the street credit that goes with rap videos and fast cars, to the truth of the violence.

I also think about Yolanda Holmes. Her salon, her generosity, her belief in her son. And how in the end, that belief became the weapon used against her. I believe in honoring her memory by telling her story—and by telling it right.

Finally, I think about the role we play. My role. Every call, every alert, every interview... They matter. The arrest of Qaw'mane, Spencer, Loriana... that was one of the harder ones. Not because it was tough to investigate, though it was. It was hard because it forced me to look into humanity's worst choices and to stand firm in the belief that justice matters.

***

The streets of Chicago will keep turning. Another homicide. Another shift. But some of these cases have truly changed me. They've reminded me that the badge I wear stands for more than law enforcement. It stands for honor, for service, and for speaking for those who have no voice.

As I write these final words of *Model Detective*—the title inspired by the producer of the WGN morning news show who saw me at a press conference and asked me, "Are you a model or a detective?"—I reflect on my journey: from young detective to experienced sergeant, from early mornings on the midnight shift to the moments where I walked out of interview rooms, knowing we'd won.

Because someone had to win. We cannot forget about the victims. Every single one of the victims I've stood over deserve justice. Their families and loved ones deserve justice. I'll leave my station lights on for the next mother, the next family, the next case. Because this job never ends.

— Michele Wood, CPD Homicide Detective Sergeant